WEIGHT WATCHERS®

WEIGHT STAGES

WEIGHT STAGES

Successfully Manage

Your Weight

Through Life's Ups and Downs

IDG Books Worldwide, Inc.
An International Data Group Company
FOSTER CITY, CA ► CHICAGO, IL ► INDIANAPOLIS, IN ► NEW YORK, NY

IDG Books Worldwide, Inc.
An International Data Group Company
919 E. Hillsdale Boulevard
Suite 400
Foster City, CA 94404

The IDG Books Worldwide logo is a registered trademark under exclusive license
to IDG Books Worldwide, Inc., from International Data Group, Inc.

WEIGHT WATCHERS is a registered trademark of
Weight Watchers International, Inc.

For general information on IDG Books Worldwide's books in the U.S.,
please call our Consumer Customer Service department at 800-762-2974.
For reseller information, including discounts and premium sales, please call our
Reseller Customer Service department at 800-434-3422.

Cataloging-in-Publication Data available from the Library of Congress

ISBN: 0-02-863705-4

A Word about Weight Watchers

Since 1963, Weight Watchers has grown from a handful of people to millions of
enrollments annually. Today, Weight Watchers is recognized as the leading name in safe
and sensible weight control. Weight Watchers members form a diverse group, from
youths to senior citizens, attending meetings virtually around the globe. Weight-loss and
weight-management results vary by individual, but we recommend that you attend
Weight Watchers meetings, follow the Weight Watchers food plan, and participate in
regular physical activity. For the Weight Watchers meeting nearest you,
call 1-800-651-6000. Or visit us at our website at www.weightwatchers.com.

Weight Watchers Publishing Group

Creative & Editorial Director: Nancy Gagliardi
Senior Editor: Christine Senft, M.S.
Publishing Assistant: Jenny Laboy-Brace

Writer: Stacey Colino, M.S.J.

Cover and book design: Michele Laseau
Illustrations: Michele Laseau

Manufactured in the United States of America

10 9 8 7 6 5 4 3 2

Contents

Acknowledgments

With special thanks to Weight Watchers Scientific Advisory Council members:

Michael Lowe, Ph.D., Professor of Psychology, MCP Hahnemann University, Philadelphia, Pennsylvania

Roland Weinsier, M.D., Ph.D., Professor and Chairman, Department of Nutrition Sciences, University of Alabama at Birmingham

We would also like to thank the following researchers and experts who added invaluable insight:

John Foreyt, Ph.D., Director of the Nutrition Research Clinic, Baylor College of Medicine, Houston, Texas

Barbara Gower, Ph.D., Assistant Professor, Department of Nutrition Sciences, Division of Physiology and Metabolism, University of Alabama at Birmingham

Ann Kearney-Cooke, Ph.D., Director, Cincinnati Psychotherapy Institute

Harry Lando, Ph.D., Professor, Division of Epidemiology, School of Public Health, University of Minnesota, Minneapolis

Janet Laubgross, Ph.D., psychologist, weight management, Fairfax, Virginia

Laurey Simkin-Silverman, Ph.D., Assistant Professor of Epidemiology, Psychiatry, and Health Services Administration, University of Pittsburgh

Mark Vander Weg, Ph.D., Research Assistant Professor, University of Memphis Prevention Center

Wayne Westcott, Ph.D., fitness research director at the South Shore YMCA in Quincy, Massachusetts

Body Mass Index Chart (pages 4–5) from *Clinical Guidelines on the Evaluation and Treatment of Overweight and Obesity in Adults: The Evidence Report*, National Heart, Lung and Blood Institute, National Institutes of Health, U.S. Department of Health and Human Services, Public Health Service, NIH Pub. No. 98-4083, September 1998

Classic Pizzelles

6 eggs
3½ cups flour
1½ cups sugar
2 Tbsp. vanilla or anise

1 cup margarine, melted (do
not use more or substitute oil)
4 tsp. baking powder

Beat eggs, adding sugar gradually. Beat until smooth.

Add cooled margarine and vanilla or anise.

Sift flour and baking powder.

Blend into egg mixture until smooth. Dough will be sticky enough to be dropped by spoon.

Bake in Pizzelle Baker. Makes approximately 60 pizzelles.

VARIATION: PIZZELLES WITH NUTS. Finely chop one cup of walnuts or pecans. Blend into Classic Pizzelle dough.

Chocolate Pizzelles

2 cup cocoa
cup sugar

½ tsp. baking powder

ft cocoa, additional sugar and baking powder into dry ingre-
nts for Classic Pizzelles.

nd into egg mixture until smooth. Makes approximatley 60
colate pizzelles.

ing Hint: Pizzelles provide the base for a delicious ice
sandwich. Can also be rolled and filled with desired fill-
r a perfect dessert.

◼ VITANTONIO. COOKWARE FOR A NEW TRADITION ◼

Vitantonio is a well-known name in kitchens where cooking in the old style is an art for today. Our product line is full of bright ideas—from baking irons to espresso machines, tools for making pasta and pizza, canned foods and desserts—guaranteed to stir your imagination and satisfy your tastes for both tradition and convenience.

Your new **Pizzelle Baker** is crafted with care in America and bears the symbol of safety for home use.

 110-120 volts A.C.

1/2

Si
die

Ble
choc

Serv
cream
ings f

Introduction

Are you in a Weight Stage? If you've picked up this book, you probably are.

Almost every woman has experienced one. Weight Stages are those self-defining times of your life that can shuffle and rearrange how you view the world, your body, and ultimately, yourself. For instance, an initial Weight Stage might be college or the first time you're left to navigate the world, your eating habits, and your body on your own. For others, a first Weight Stage might be prompted by the exchange of wedding rings or embarking on the nine-month rollercoaster ride toward motherhood. Other Weight Stages might be more subtle, such as when you're ready to take control of your health (by quitting smoking) or your life (such as getting through a divorce). And there is, of course, that universal Weight Stage that countless women encounter at a time when they're probably most comfortable—and at peace—with their bodies: menopause. All these Stages can be exhilarating, challenging, and ultimately, life-enhancing—yet they also have the potential of wreaking havoc on your self-esteem and weight.

Weight Watchers Weight Stages: Successfully Manage Your Weight Through Life's Ups and Downs explores the most common life-altering events, or Stages, that can play a role in your weight. This book is designed to give you a clear picture of the physical and psychological events that can happen at each Stage; explain what's happening; and then provide clear, concise ideas and information on how to best manage the Stage without gaining weight.

We suggest that you use *Weight Watchers Weight Stages* as a reference book. Leaf through the pages and read about the Weight Stage you might be in right now—but don't limit yourself to the present. Even if you're well past your college years or haven't yet experienced the joy of motherhood, don't dismiss the power of your past or fear the uncertainty of the future. These chapters can help you better understand why you reacted the way you did in a situation or prepare you for what's to come.

Be sure to pass this book on—to your daughter, a relative or friend. Chances are, she may be going through a particular Weight Stage and craves insight into understanding the whys of weight gain—and the knowledge of how to prevent it. And with that knowledge, ultimately, comes the power to enable a woman to take charge of her life.

Nancy Gagliardi
CREATIVE & EDITORIAL DIRECTOR

A Dieting Life

Wouldn't it be nice if the tables could be turned for just a little while? If women could sit back and, rather than having to worry about gaining weight at various stages of our lives, actually lose weight more easily as we got older? If we didn't feel the need to

continuously scrutinize the circumference of our thighs or the extra padding on our derrieres—and fret about how to get rid of the excess as quickly as possible? If we didn't have to reckon with societal pressure to achieve a certain body ideal that's virtually impossible for most of us to attain? Maybe that's the way it is in some parallel universe, but not on earth.

The unfortunate truth is this: At one time or another, most women find themselves struggling to lose weight or to come to terms with their changing shapes, much more so than men do. At any given time, 40 percent of women in the U.S. are trying to lose weight, compared to 25 percent of men who are trying to slim down. What's more, a 1995 study found that across all ages, a higher percentage of women than men gain or lose weight of any amount. And yet despite the national obsession with fitness and fat-free packaged foods, research shows that we're getting fatter and fatter with every decade. Worse, women typically gain weight over a longer period of their lives than men do.

According to the latest definition of what it means to be "overweight"—having a body mass index (BMI) between 25 and 29.9—more American women are considered overweight than ever before. (To calculate your BMI, see chart, pages 4–5.)

Similarly, more American women are now considered obese—which is now defined as having a body mass index of 30 or greater—than in the past. At this point, too, a higher percentage of women than men in the U.S. are now considered obese—25 percent of American women, compared to 20 percent of men.

Even more disturbing is the fact that the prevalence of being overweight or obese goes up decade by decade among women until the age of 60, when it begins to decline. Among women in their twenties, 33 percent are now considered overweight or obese. This figure rises to 47 percent with women in their thirties; 53 percent with women in their forties; and 64 percent with women in their fifties.

Carrying around extra pounds doesn't just take a toll on your appearance. It threatens your health, too. In fact, obesity contributes to the development of many serious conditions, including hypertension, diabetes, heart disease, and cancer. In addition, excess weight is associated with sleep apnea—a disorder in which breathing stops during sleep—and gallbladder disease, as well as bone, joint, and back problems. And because it puts a lot of wear and tear on your body, it can be a less-than-obvious cause of fatigue, breathing difficulties, and everyday aches and pains. Moreover, obesity has been found to negatively affect menstruation and fertility by wreaking havoc on a woman's balance of hormones.

Fortunately, many of these risks decrease substantially when a woman loses a modest amount of weight. Researchers from the Centers for Disease Control and Prevention analyzed data from more than 43,000 overweight women and found that intentional weight loss led to a 25 percent reduction in the risk of premature death from heart disease, cancer, and other health-related causes; among those with obesity-related health conditions, losing any amount of weight was associated with a 20 percent drop in the risk of premature death from all causes, including a 40 to 50 percent reduction in the risk of dying from cancer and a 30 to 40 percent drop in the odds of dying from diabetes. Furthermore, losing just 10 percent of your weight if you fall under the definition of "obese" is effective in improving menstrual function, ovulation, and pregnancy rates.

What makes women loosen their grip on weight control with the passing years? A variety of factors seems to conspire to have this effect. And let's be honest: It's pretty easy to gain weight—all it takes is eating too much food and exercising too little, and suddenly you may not like what you see on the scale or in the mirror. Beyond eating and exercise, however, there are other reasons women gain weight. Some of these have to do with specific stages in a woman's life, but genetics, metabolism, environmental

Find Your Body Mass Index

	Body Mass Index (BMI)							
	19	20	21	22	23	24	25	26
58	91	96	100	105	110	115	119	124
59	94	99	104	109	114	119	124	128
60	97	102	107	112	118	123	128	133
61	100	106	111	116	122	127	132	137
62	104	109	115	120	126	131	136	142
63	107	113	118	124	130	135	141	146
64	110	116	122	128	134	140	145	151
65	114	120	126	132	138	144	150	156
66	118	124	130	136	142	148	155	161
67	121	127	134	140	146	153	159	166
68	125	131	138	144	151	158	164	171
69	128	135	142	149	155	162	169	176
70	132	139	146	153	160	167	174	181
71	136	143	150	157	165	172	179	186
72	140	147	154	162	169	177	184	191
73	144	151	159	166	174	182	189	197
74	148	155	163	171	179	186	194	202
75	152	160	168	176	184	192	200	208
76	156	164	172	180	189	197	205	213

Height (inches)

Weight

To use this table, find the appropriate height in the left-hand column. Move across to a given weight. (Pounds have been rounded off.) The number at the top of the column is the BMI at that height and weight.

27	28	29	30	31	32	33	34	35
129	134	138	143	148	153	158	162	167
133	138	143	148	153	158	163	168	173
138	143	148	153	158	163	168	174	179
143	148	153	158	164	169	174	180	185
147	153	158	164	169	175	180	186	191
152	158	163	169	175	180	186	191	197
157	163	169	174	180	186	192	197	204
162	168	174	180	186	192	198	204	210
167	173	179	186	192	198	204	210	216
172	178	185	191	198	204	211	217	223
177	184	190	197	203	210	216	223	230
182	189	196	203	209	216	223	230	236
188	195	202	209	216	222	229	236	243
193	200	208	215	222	229	236	243	250
199	206	213	221	228	235	242	250	258
204	212	219	227	235	242	250	257	265
210	218	225	233	241	249	256	264	272
216	224	232	240	248	256	264	272	279
221	230	238	246	254	263	271	279	287

factors, changes in lifestyle habits (such as giving up smoking), and emotional issues can also affect how much you eat and when.

Why You Weigh What You Weigh

If both of your parents are (or were) overweight, there's a very strong likelihood that you will be too. Whether this familial tendency toward being heavy has more to do with nature or nurture is still a matter of debate. Yes, genetic influences do seem to play a role in a person's propensity to gain weight. It appears, for example, that some genes influence how quickly a person burns calories, whereas other genes affect a person's appetite, her preferences for sweets or high-fat foods, or her ability to tell when she's full. But some of these effects are hard to separate from environmental factors.

After all, your eating habits were formed when you were young, and they were undoubtedly influenced by your parents' choices. In a 1999 study, researchers at Pennsylvania State University examined the link between the family environment and childhood obesity. What they found is that a mother's dietary disinhibition—her lack of eating restraint, in other words—and her body mass index were positive predictors that her daughter would be overweight, and a mother's level of disinhibition appeared to be independently associated with the degree to which both mother and daughter were overweight. So clearly, genetics *and* environment affect a woman's odds of being heavy.

Of course, your personal metabolism also affects how quickly you burn calories—and hence, your tendency to gain or lose weight. You might feel like you gain weight by just looking at a box of chocolates, whereas your husband may be able to eat a candy bar every day for a snack and not gain an ounce. Unfair as this is, it is due, at least in part, to your metabolic differences—your gender-related metabolic differences and your personal ones, too.

Many weight-control experts subscribe to the idea that everybody is born with a personal set point for weight, a built-in, predetermined weight range that the body will work hard to maintain. If the theory is true, the good news is that this set point makes it easier for your body to return to its weight comfort-zone after you've overeaten during the holidays, for example. Your metabolism speeds up for a time to burn off those extra calories. On the other hand, this set point also may make it difficult to reach your desired weight, which might be lower than what your body is naturally inclined to maintain. The reason: In this case, your metabolism slows down to conserve energy when you eat too little.

Thankfully, your body may be able to adjust its set point from time to time, if you increase or decrease your calorie intake or increase or decrease the amount of exercise you get. Which means if you decrease your caloric intake and/or increase your exercise, you can lose weight. Once your weight stabilizes at its new level, your body will then establish a new set point that it will fiercely hold onto once again.

The Ages and Stages of a Woman's Weight

One of the reasons women struggle with their weight more than men do is because we have a higher percentage of body fat—at any age. Women have, on average, 23 percent body fat, whereas men have 16 percent body fat. From the start of adolescence, girls typically gain fat and muscle, but it's the fat that's often most noticeable—and often most disliked—in their breasts, hips, thighs, and buttocks. This is functional fat because it prepares girls for menstruation—and, later, for pregnancy and lactation. The body is hard-wired to store fat in these areas because these are the most accessible sites from which to draw fat for reproductive-related functions such as breastfeeding.

Plus, as we get older, we typically tend to get fatter as we lose lean muscle mass. In her twenties, a woman will lose, on average, three pounds of muscle per decade. Between the ages of 30 and 50, a woman will lose, on average, at least five pounds of muscle per decade. And between the ages of 50 and 60, women typically lose ten pounds of muscle. At the same time, her percentage of body fat increases with each decade. Even if a

Your Heritage, Your Weight

It's long been known that certain ethnic groups are more prone to obesity than others and seem to have more trouble losing weight. According to the latest data, 49 percent of white women are currently overweight or obese, 66 percent of black women are, and 66 percent of Mexican American women are. By contrast, research from an HMO in northern California found that only 22 percent of Asian American women are considered overweight.

Just what accounts for these ethnic differences isn't known for sure, although eating and exercise patterns likely play a role. But new research also suggests that there may be metabolic variations among ethnic groups. Some studies have shown, for example, that resting metabolic rate—the number of calories a person burns at rest—is lower among obese African American women than among obese white women. And a 1999 study from the University of Pennsylvania School of Medicine found that these differences don't disappear but actually magnify with weight loss. After participating in a six-month weight-loss program, the African American women's metabolic rate dropped even further than the white women's did— by 10 percent, compared to 6 percent. Both groups of women did lose weight, but the underlying message is that it may be more difficult for African American women—and perhaps for those of other ethnic origins—to lose weight and maintain a lower weight.

This may help to explain why African American women tend to lose less weight than white women do in weight-control programs. It also may explain why African American women often woman didn't gain an ounce on the scale during her entire adult life—a most unlikely occurrence—she would notice a shift in the distribution of fat on her body. She'd also probably notice a difference in her shape, since body fat is considerably bulkier than the same weight of muscle is. So by losing muscle and

gain more weight during pregnancy and have a harder time losing the extra pounds afterward. Indeed, a 1995 study from the University of South Carolina found that after pregnancy African American women retained, on average, six pounds more than white women did.

But here's a real surprise: The health-related risks of being overweight aren't democratic across ethnic groups. For example, a 1998 study from the University of North Carolina, Chapel Hill, examined the association between body mass index (BMI) and mortality rates from heart disease and other causes among white and African American women. While BMI was positively associated with mortality rates from both heart disease and other causes for both groups, the thresholds varied considerably. Among women who had never smoked, there was a 40 percent higher risk of dying prematurely among white women with a BMI of 27.3, whereas that same risk increase applied to African American women with a BMI of 35.9. Which means that when it comes to health risks, BMI may be a less potent variable for African American women than it is for white women.

So depending on your ethnic or racial background, you may have a harder or easier time losing weight than other women do. By the same token, you may need to lose more or less weight to reduce the health risks that are associated with being overweight. Which goes to show, with some matters of the body, you just have to play with the cards you're dealt.

gaining fat, a woman can gain inches and dress sizes, if not pounds.

All of these changes are significant because each pound of muscle burns 35 to 50 calories a day while you're resting, whereas a pound of body fat burns only 2 calories a day. So losing muscle mass doesn't just change your body's tone; it *can* lead to unwanted pounds too, because your metabolism will slow down. If you eat the same number of calories as you always did, you'll gain weight as you lose muscle, unless you start increasing the amount of time you spend exercising.

This is just one of the reasons why adults tend to gain an average of half a pound to one pound per year through adulthood. Another reason has to do with fluctuations in reproductive hormones that occur throughout women's lives, a factor that predisposes us to weight gain. For example, research involving both animals and women has found that hormonal changes during the menstrual cycle affect calorie intake as well as resting metabolic rate. During the luteal phase of the menstrual cycle, typically days 15 to 25, a woman's body often produces heat in response to the hormone progesterone, which results in more energy being expended throughout the day. As a result, a woman's body needs an additional 100 to 300 calories a day during this time, which most women naturally consume without thinking about it. But this does explain why many women feel hungrier at this time of the month.

In addition, the hormonal changes brought by pregnancy naturally lead to weight gain, which is normal and healthy during the nine months. But many women end up gaining excessive amounts of weight during pregnancy, which can set them up for further weight gain down the road. Many women hold on to five pounds or more after a given pregnancy, which they never lose. Several factors seem to play a role in determining how much weight a woman is likely to retain after having a baby. The amount of weight she gains during pregnancy is the most significant factor, but her dietary patterns, how long she waits between pregnancies, how soon she returns to work, her ethnic heritage, and, of course, genetics can also affect what registers on the scale after the postpartum period. And if a woman retains an extra five pounds from one pregnancy going into the next, the pounds can steadily creep onto her body with each child.

During menopause, which signifies the end of a woman's reproductive life, many women typically gain up to five pounds, according to research. Weight gain at this time of life is linked with a decrease in physical activity, which often occurs with advancing age. But some of it may also reflect the fact that fat begins to accumulate in the waist and abdomen as a result of the drop in estrogen. This is yet another pivotal stage in a woman's life where she's at risk for gaining excessive amounts of weight—unless she pays close attention to her eating and exercise habits.

Meanwhile, as people move from one phase of their lives to the next, they naturally tend to become more sedentary as they get older. For example, after getting married and moving to the suburbs, some women may cut back on even short bouts of exercise because they begin living the commuter's life. Similarly, mothers of young children may find it difficult to squeeze in time to exercise. For others, long hours spent sitting behind a desk can decrease the number of calories they burn through physical activity during the day. Whatever is at the root of this inactivity, research has found that even small decreases in energy expenditure can add up to considerable weight gain. In a 1993 study, for example, researchers from the University of Alabama at Birmingham found that burning up 50 to 200 fewer calories per day than one needs can lead a lean woman to gradually gain anywhere from 7 to 33 pounds within ten years.

Your Self-Reflection

While these biological changes are taking place throughout a woman's life span, a woman's body image tends to be more vulnerable at certain stages of her life—especially during adolescence, pregnancy, the postpartum period, and menopause. Not surprisingly, these reproductive milestones coincide with the body's natural inclination to add body fat, which is in direct opposition to many women's appearance and weight-related goals. So women may be emotionally at odds with their bodies during certain phases of life, which can set them up for emotional eating.

Cultural standards are also a driving force behind a negative body image, which can affect a woman's dieting history. While the female form has hardly changed a bit since the days of Adam and Eve, the cultural ideal of beauty has swung wildly from one body type to another over the years. (This has hardly been the case for men's physiques.) In the mid-1800s, the curvy hourglass figure reigned supreme—large breasts and hips, with tightly corseted waists, were the order of the day. Fast-forward to the 1900s, and we saw the "ideal woman" transform from the slim, flat-chested flapper of the 1920s to the comeback of curves (à la Marilyn Monroe) in the 1950s, which gave way to Twiggy in the 1960s. In the 1990s alone, the female figures in vogue have ranged from the sculpted athletic form of, say, supermodel Cindy Crawford to the waif look of model Kate Moss.

Given that women have tried to alter their bodies to conform to the current definition of attractiveness, it's no wonder body-image problems are rampant among them. Some surveys have found that as many as 85 percent of American women are unhappy with at least some aspect of their bodies. And research from the University of South Florida has found that more than 95 percent of women overestimate their body size, guessing that they are on average 25 percent larger than they really are. Feeling bad about your body can have a profound impact on your health and well-being. Research has found, for example, that body-image disturbances are linked to eating disorders, low self-esteem, anxiety, loneliness, and depression, among other ills. (For more about the psychological traps that can affect weight, see chapter two.) All of these factors can influence your eating and exercise habits—and, hence, your weight. And since biological factors, especially genetics, significantly affect a woman's body shape and the regulation of her body weight, the current ideal for the perfect body—one that is very thin and physically fit—may be absolutely unattainable. This sets up a collision between culture and physiology, one that can influence how a woman feels about and treats her body throughout her life.

How to Use This Book

We may not be able to change the fact that society holds women to unfair standards of beauty—or that it's easier for women to gain weight than it is for men. But with any luck, this book will serve as a valuable reference tool or road map for the millions of women who deal with weight issues at some time in their lives. Chances are, only one or two of the chapters will apply to your life at any given time, so you may not read this book in one sitting.

But hold onto it; it's a guide worth keeping forever. Why? Because it's all about the stages and situations in a woman's life where she's most at risk for losing control of her weight. Because it will alert you to the weight-related traps that you could fall into sooner or later—whether it's during pregnancy, marriage, or menopause, or while enduring job stress or a major move across the country. And because with many of these stages and situations, there's a cumulative effect. Trying to quit smoking right before or during menopause can lead to greater weight gain, for example. And relocating to another part of the country shortly after having a baby could set you up for a greater loss of control over your eating and exercise habits.

You also may want to pass this book on to your daughter, perhaps as she enters college, to help her avoid some of the struggles you may have encountered. At the end of this book you'll find a chapter called "The Secrets of Staying Slim at Any Stage of

Life," which is full of strategies and a two-week meal plan to help you manage your weight anytime, anywhere. Armed with the knowledge contained in these pages and strategies to help you avoid unhealthy lifestyle habits, you'll increase your chances of controlling your weight and preserving your health over the decades.

What Are the Weight Stages?

It probably won't surprise you to hear that biology alone doesn't drive you to eat. You probably knew that already based on your own personal experience. It's true that you eat in order to provide your body with an adequate intake of nutrients to stay alive

and perform basic bodily functions, such as breathing, digesting, sleeping, and so on. And it's true that your body does require greater or fewer calories to fulfill these needs at different times of your life. Hunger—that gnawing feeling that occurs in the pit of your stomach after you haven't eaten for a few hours—is what signals your brain that it's time to refuel, alerting your brain that your body needs more nutrients for energy and maintenance. But beyond these physiological triggers for eating are a variety of emotional and psychological issues that can send you to the refrigerator or pantry between meals.

After all, the act of eating can numb unpleasant feelings; it's a distraction, a source of comfort. But if you have a tendency to use food as a way to manage emotions—particularly when you feel emotionally upset or unnerved—you may struggle with your weight throughout your life. This is especially true if eating as a form of self-soothing behavior was something you learned in your family of origin, as many people do; if the habit goes back that far, it's deeply rooted, perhaps even an automatic response by now. If you find yourself noshing as you try to cope with the usual ups and downs of everyday life, certain periods of your life may be particularly challenging when stress, anxiety, depression, or agitation begin to color your world. Or when you begin to struggle emotionally with the reality of your changing body during pregnancy or menopause, for example.

By now, you have a sense of how the physiological changes your body will endure throughout your life can affect your size and shape. But biology is hardly destiny when it comes to weight management. It can make you more vulnerable to gaining weight at certain points in your life, but it's your habits that will or won't send you in that direction. And at the root of your habits, there are bound to be psychological or emotional factors that can influence whether you're likely to gain or lose weight during those taxing times. It's not that these psychological issues have a direct effect on your weight but rather that they affect your eating and exercise practices. In a 1998 study, researchers from Wesleyan University in Middletown, Connecticut, examined women's and men's beliefs about why they gained weight, and they found that women rated depression, stress, low self-esteem, and a need to avoid certain situations as more significant reasons for their weight gain than men did. Not only that, but after losing weight, women were more likely to feel terrible about overeating or slacking off on exercise, and they'd regain much of the weight they'd lost in response to these feelings.

Stress can have an especially potent effect on women, many of whom are restrained eaters, meaning they feel that they need to consciously restrict their food intake in order to prevent weight gain. Research has found, for example, that restrained eating among women predicts vulnerability to stress-related overeating. And since 40 percent of women in the U.S. are trying to lose weight at any given time, it looks like stress affects the eating habits of a significant number of women. In a 1998 study, researchers from the University of British Columbia examined stress-induced eating behavior among women by making them feel stressed out—this stressed-out state was confirmed by physiological measures of heart rate and blood pressure—then making food inconspicuously available as they recovered. Not surprisingly, women who didn't normally restrict their eating habits ate less food when they were stressed out than did those who typically exercised dietary restraint. Indeed, other research has found that among restrained eaters, stress can be like floodgates opening for food. All control gets tossed out the window as these women indulge in an emotionally driven feeding frenzy.

So what makes a particular stage or situation in life especially treacherous when it comes to controlling your eating habits and your weight? Basically, a Weight Stage is a phase of your life or a set of circumstances in which a variety of biological, emotional, or behavioral factors seem to conspire to make you gain weight. In short, these various influences can alter your metabolic rate and/or your eating and exercise habits in such a way that your body is susceptible to gaining weight. Many of these factors involve mood fluctuations or changes in body image, both of which can lead to emotionally fueled eating in an effort to soothe yourself. Others have more to do with the stress of adjusting to new demands that are placed upon you—whether they stem from getting married, having a baby, or starting a new job, for instance.

Still other factors may be linked to feelings of loneliness—if you've recently moved to a new town or if you're stuck in an unhappy marriage, for example. Indeed, loneliness is often a major trigger for emotional overeating; filling yourself up with food can create the illusion of filling the void within. In a sense, food can become a lonely person's best friend, her trusted companion, but it can also betray her, as it leads to unwanted pounds. A woman's uncertainty about the future—resulting from the addition of a new family member or the fact that grown children have recently left home—can also incite the urge to eat for comfort, as a way of calming herself as she tries to cope with these changes.

By influencing a woman's eating habits, all of these psychological or emotional issues can take a toll on a woman's weight. Granted, the weight-related changes engendered by these Weight Stages don't happen overnight but generally over a period of weeks, months, perhaps even years. Here's a glimpse of some of the riskiest periods in a woman's life, as far as weight-control goes.

The College Years: Enrolling in a college or university often marks a woman's first brush with independent living, a flight to freedom from parental rules and regulations—and that's true of food choices, too. For the first time in your life, you can eat what you want when you want—without being scolded by your mother, father, or other family members. But faced with the responsibility of having to choose your own breakfast, lunch, dinner, and snacks, you may not always make the smartest food choices or exercise portion control in a dining hall that offers unlimited choices. And with the typically erratic schedules of college life—alternating class times, late nights spent studying, exam crunch periods, and so on—your eating habits can become highly irregular. This can affect your metabolism for the worse and set you up for overeating at irregular meals, and for noshing late at night while you're studying or after going out to parties with your friends. Plus, the student's life is often quite sedentary. Research has found that fewer than 40 percent of college students engage in vigorous activity three or more days per week. Add to these factors the stress of exams and academic competition and the emotional highs and lows that often come from being away from home for the first extended period of time, and it's no wonder many college women often end up eating for emotional reasons. It's also no surprise that many college students gain 10 or more pounds during the freshman year alone. But it is possible to graduate from one year to the next without adding pounds, and chapter three will show you how.

Tying the Knot: It's one of those secrets your married friends don't tell you about before you walk down the aisle: After saying their "I do's," both men and women are likely to gain weight, but women appear to be at greater risk for adding pounds in the more immediate future. Research has found, for example, that during the newlywed period women gain an average of five pounds over the course of the year, whereas men don't experience any significant weight change during this period. And with each passing anniversary, the gaining trend is likely to continue. Much of this conjugal weight gain stems from lifestyle changes. Women may be changing their eating habits to match their husbands' after they get married; they may be eating larger portions, heavier foods, or more frequent meals or snacks. Plus, many people become less physically active after they marry because they'd rather spend time with each other than at the gym. But part of this marriage-related weight gain is probably tied to psychological issues. Maybe you've relaxed the strict eating and exercise standards you once imposed on yourself now that you no longer have to compete in the singles' world; maybe now that you feel so loved and accepted, weight control doesn't seem as important; maybe you find yourself struggling emotionally with the role of being a spouse, or maybe you find yourself eating for emotional reasons if you don't end up living as happily ever after as you'd hoped. In chapter four, you'll read about the weight-related traps that married women typically fall into and learn strategies on how to steer clear of them.

Having a Baby: Of course, you're *supposed* to gain weight during pregnancy, but many women go overboard. Some expectant mothers figure that since they're eating for two, they might as well give in wholeheartedly, so they begin eating extra-large portions at meals and snacks whenever they feel like it. Others feel that with all the changes that are happening to their bodies, they're entitled to eat whatever they want, especially if they feel deprived because they've given up caffeine, alcohol, or cigarettes for the baby's sake. A woman also may struggle with body-image issues. After a lifetime spent scrutinizing the size and shape of her body, she may feel emotionally at odds with her growing girth and physically uncomfortable moving around, which can trigger stress-related eating. Likewise, worries about how having a baby will change their lives and their marriages can drive expectant mothers to eat in an effort to provide self-comfort and self-nurturing. Meanwhile, physical discomfort or lack of motivation can cause many mothers-to-be to become more sedentary during these nine months. Given these myriad influences, it's no wonder many women gain excessive amounts of weight during pregnancy. And with all the physical and emotional adjustments that are required during the postpartum months, this is often a difficult time for women to start exercising regularly or to shape up their eating habits. So it's hardly surprising that women often retain two to eight extra pounds a year after giving birth. You can get through pregnancy without sabotaging your figure, however, and chapter five will guide you in the right direction.

On-the-Job Stress: Stress has become a fact of the modern working life, regardless of what line of work you're in. It may stem from long hours, deadline pressure, too much responsibility, too little control, unreasonable colleagues or bosses, competition, pay inequities, or corporate cutbacks, but wherever it comes from, there's no question that the world of work is rife with stress these days. And if you're prone to stress-related eating, work-related pressure can take a toll on your weight. Research has found, for example, that having a highly demanding job is associated with higher body mass index among women. Meanwhile, working under the threat or possibility of losing your job can lead many women to gain weight, according to studies. While these effects undoubtedly involve stress-related eating, other factors also play a role. For example, the way we work has become increasingly sedentary over the years, and while spending long hours sitting behind your desk may earn you points with your boss or even a promotion, it can make finding time to exercise regularly difficult. It can also make it challenging to plan and eat regular, healthy meals—or to resist the lure of the office vending machine while you're working late. Now for the good news: If you want to develop or maintain a brilliant career, you can do so without gaining weight. Chapter six offers a plan to help you maintain a healthy lifestyle and emotional habits even in the face of job stress.

Moving to a New Home or a New City: Research has found that moving ranks right up there among life's most stressful events. And if you're not entirely happy about the change in locale or if the process of packing up and moving becomes overly burdensome, it may feel even more stressful. Plus, when you're pulling up roots, you end up losing much of the immediate social support you may have come to rely upon. As a result, you may find yourself seeking comfort in a pint of Rocky Road when you feel lonely or overwhelmed by your changing circumstances. Also influencing your lifestyle habits is the fact that while you're moving, life tends to go through a period without structure. Your new surroundings may be unfamiliar, so you may not know where to shop or where to exercise, for example. To save time and minimize inconvenience while you're unpacking, you may end up grabbing fast food on the run or ordering take-out, which aren't the best choices for weight control. As you and your family try to settle into your new home and attempt to develop some sort of routine, eating healthfully or exercising regularly may not seem very important. Unless you're careful, however, this tendency to shirk healthy habits could continue, in which case it could lead to considerable weight gain. In chapter seven, you'll discover the sneaky factors that can compromise healthy eating and exercise habits while you're moving. You'll also learn how to seize control in

Psychological Well-Being and Weight Change

When it comes to a woman's emotional well-being, gaining or losing weight can exert a powerful influence. It can affect everything from how she sees herself to how she feels about herself to how she treats herself. Not surprisingly, a study of more than 3,700 women by researchers at the National Center for Health Statistics found that recent weight gain was linked with poorer psychological well-being in women who were overweight, as well as in those who weren't.

But surprisingly enough, the opposite effect has also been presumed to be true: that losing weight is also associated with poorer psychological well-being in women. The theory is that food restriction places the body in starvation mode physically and leads to psychological disturbances, including depression, an obsession with food, and overeating (or binge eating). But a recent review of studies disputes this idea rather convincingly. The researchers found no evidence that dieting through a weight-loss program leads to a downturn in mood; on the contrary, most of the studies found that mood improved, regardless of how much weight participants lost. In particular, it appears that programs that incorporate behavioral measures such as small ways so that this period of adjustment doesn't lead to weight gain.

Giving Up Cigarettes: Without a doubt, smoking is a tough habit to kick, especially since many women use it as a way to control their weight. For many women, smoking helps them eat less, perhaps because it blunts their appetite and their sense of taste. Others are concerned about gaining weight if they do kick the habit, which is legitimate since nicotine also increases a person's metabolic rate, at least in the short term. Not only is smoking physically addictive, but it can be psychologically addictive, too,

coping strategies and encourage exercise actually provide plenty of feel-good benefits.

What's more, a recent study found that women participating in a Weight Watchers program—which involved increasing physical activity, eating a lower-calorie diet, and partaking of group support—experienced improvements in overall mood, feelings of self-worth, and body satisfaction after 12 weeks. These women also scored higher in measures of quality of life and self-confidence than did those in a control group. Not only can this make a woman feel better about herself and her entire life, but research also has found that improved psychological well-being has been associated with an increased likelihood of weight-loss maintenance.

The bottom line is this: Whether losing weight will have a negative impact on your emotional well-being depends largely on how you try to shed pounds. As with most things in life, there's a right way and a wrong way to do it. And the evidence seems to suggest that by taking a moderate approach to weight loss—one that includes reasonable calorie reductions rather than drastic ones, along with regular exercise and support from others—it is possible to lose excess weight and feel good, too.

since cigarettes have the unusual power to calm people down when they're upset or rev them up when they're tired. So the habit becomes a way of managing stress for many people. In other words, cigarettes often become an emotional crutch, just as favorite foods are for other people. When they quit smoking, however, many women struggle with physical withdrawal and emotional cravings for comfort, which are often fulfilled by eating favorite—especially sweet—foods. Research has found, for example, that people consistently consume 250 to 350 more calories per day after they quit smoking. Which makes perfect sense, given that women often gain up to ten pounds after they kick the habit. It doesn't have to be this way, though. You can stub out the habit permanently without extinguishing your weight-control efforts. Chapter eight outlines the troublesome situations you're likely to encounter as you try to quit smoking and provides strategies for how to handle them without adding pounds.

The Midlife Change: During menopause, the final milestone in a woman's reproductive life, the dropoff in estrogen does bring about an increase in body fat in the abdominal region. Whether it also leads to weight gain is still a matter of debate, although there's some suggestion that when estrogen diminishes, appetite may increase. While it's not clear what all the underlying causes are, research has found that the average woman gains two to five pounds during the entire menopausal transition; some women gain considerably more, however. What is well established is that as people get older, they tend to become more sedentary, and this is especially true of women. With a more sedentary lifestyle comes a loss of muscle mass and an increase in body fat, and these changes, in turn, cause a downturn in a woman's metabolic rate, making it easier for her to gain weight. For some women, the emotional adjustments that accompany menopause can also lead to weight gain. If a woman struggles with depression, with the reality that her children have grown up, with self-image or identity issues, or with a growing discomfort over her changing body, she may be susceptible to emotional eating, which can quickly lead to unwanted pounds. But it is possible to enter the next stage of your life, the one following menopause, without going up a dress size. Chapter nine will show you how to navigate through the behavioral and emotional minefields menopause can bring—without compromising your waistline, your health, or your psychological well-being.

Of course, whether you get through these Weight Stages without gaining weight is largely up to you. We can give you all the tools and strategies in the world, but it's up to you to put them into practice. Which means that you need to be committed, to really want to get through these challenging periods of your life without sabotaging your figure or your health. Throughout these chapters, you'll read stories from women who've been there—women who, like you, have struggled with these Weight Stages and found ways to beat them. Hopefully, as you get a glimpse of their experiences, you'll be able to learn from what they did right and what they did wrong. And, most likely, this will take much of the struggle out of your own encounters with these Weight Stages.

chapter Three

The College Challenge

Wendy never had a problem with her weight—until she went to college. Then, over the next four years, as she went from being an inexperienced freshman to a more worldly senior, she added nearly 20 pounds to her 5'5" frame. "During college, I developed just

about every bad eating habit in the book," confesses the New York writer, now 34. "I would eat popcorn as a meal sometimes. Other times, I would starve myself all day—I never ate breakfast back then—then I'd eat three times as much at night because I was so hungry. It would start at seven or eight o'clock at night, and my friends and I would gorge. We used to order quarts of ice cream from this great local place. We'd get one per person, and we'd eat the whole thing at midnight before we went to bed."

In addition, Wendy and her friends often fell into alcohol-related diet traps: "I'd forget that alcohol has calories, or we'd go to happy hour and eat lots of chips and free chicken wings while we were drinking," she recalls. "Then, after a night out partying, we'd go out for breakfast at 4 A.M. and get omelets, toast, the works. Afterwards, we'd go home and go to sleep with a full stomach. When I look back, I can't believe some of the things I did in college."

Gaining weight during the college years, especially the infamous Freshman 15, is legendary. Generation after generation of college students has left home in the fall and returned home the following summer 10 to 15 pounds heavier. It's such a widespread phenomenon that it has practically become a rite of passage, almost like attending freshman orientation or pledging a sorority. For other students, the weight changes don't come as quickly; they simply gain pounds gradually from the freshman through senior years. In a 1985 study, researchers compared weight changes between women enrolled at a large private university and among those of the same age from the community over three years. The college women gained a mean of .73 pounds per month during their first year—adding an average of more than 8 pounds over the course of the year—a rate that was 36 times faster than that of the comparison group from the community. (Interestingly, many of these gains were lost by the end of their junior year when many of the women chose to move off campus and no longer relied on cafeteria food services for their meals.)

Meanwhile, the 1995 National College Health Risk Behavior Survey, conducted by the Centers for Disease Control and Prevention, found that 21 percent of college students are overweight based on a body mass index (BMI) equal to or greater than 27.8 for men and 27.3 for women. The actual percentage of college students who are overweight is probably considerably higher now that the definition has changed to a BMI over 25.

Decisions, Decisions

What is it about entering college that makes people so vulnerable to gaining weight? After a lifetime of having Mom or Dad plan and prepare most of your meals for you, the sudden freedom of food choice at college can be both liberating and overwhelming, particularly if your dining hall or food service plan offers a buffet-style selection. No one's looking over your shoulder to make sure you have all the major food groups represented on your plate; for the first time in your life, you can eat what you want when you want—without being scolded by a parent. So it's hardly surprising that, faced with the responsibility of having to choose their own breakfast, lunch, dinner, and snacks, students may not always make the smartest food choices; instead, they go with what strikes their fancy at the moment. Or they may not exercise portion control as they go back for second helpings or decide to sample another—perhaps more satisfying—offering.

Yet having such a wide selection of foods from which to choose each meal can become the bane of weight control, according to new research from Tufts University in Boston. When a team of nutritionists recruited 71 healthy men and women to record the types of foods they ate over a six-month period, they found that eating a greater variety of foods—especially sweets, snacks, condiments, entrees, and carbohydrates—was linked to consuming more calories and increased body fat over the long term. The exception: People who consumed a wider variety of vegetables—the minority, to be sure—tended to be thinner.

Other research has found that college students' diets are woefully inadequate when it comes to fulfilling the guidelines from the U.S. Department of Agriculture Food Guide Pyramid. A 1998 survey of 302 students at the University of Pittsburgh found that 80 percent of the students don't consume enough grains, fruits, vegetables, and dairy products. And a 1998 study from Simmons College in Boston concluded that college women's diets are high in total and saturated fat and low in fiber, fruits, vegetables, and dairy products. Moreover, recent college students typically consumed more calories per day than previous generations did. Data from the National Nutrition Monitoring and Related Research Program shows that students who were in college between 1988 and 1991 consumed an average of 1,957 calories per day, compared to 1,675 calories per day consumed by students between 1976 and 1980.

The typically erratic schedules of college life—alternating class times, late nights spent studying, midterm and final exam crunch periods, and so on—can lead to similarly irregular eating habits. As a result, a student might skip meals—especially breakfast if she has the option of sleeping late on a particular day—then overdo it at the next meal. Or she may be forced to grab food on the run—a doughnut or a muffin here, a candy bar there, or whatever's handy—before class. Hitting the books late into the night can also stimulate a student's appetite psychologically, and what's available at those hours isn't usually the healthiest fare. You might pick up the phone and order a pizza or an ice cream sundae, or get fast food from the local drive-through with your buddies, or make a beeline for the vending machine. And before you know it, you've consumed the calorie equivalent of another meal.

The camaraderie of college life can also make you lose sight of just how much food you're actually consuming. In a 1992 study at Georgia State University, researchers instructed 30 students either to eat alone or to dine with other people over the course of three five-day periods; when the students ate with other students, they consumed more food, water, sodium, and alcohol than when they ate alone. In fact, their food intake was 60 percent higher when they dined with others than when they ate by themselves. It may be that when you get caught up in the conversation and you're enjoying the company you're with, you pay less attention to how much food you actually put in your mouth. Plus, since meals are among the most social times in a student's day, it's tempting to linger at the table and perhaps have a little more to eat to prolong the get-together.

The Sedentary Life of a Student

Between attending classes and discussion groups and spending long hours poring over books in the library, a college student's typical day can include a lot of sitting—and more sitting. There's no question, being highly studious can boost your GPA (grade point average), but it can also increase your BMI (body mass index) if you don't carve out time for exercise. It's ironic: When you're in college, you have greater and cheaper access to exercise facilities than you have ever had in your life—or ever will again. Yet many students don't take advantage of the gym, the jogging trails, or the team sports opportunities. According to the 1995 National College Health Risk Behavior Survey, only 38 percent of the nearly 5,000 students surveyed engaged in vigorous physical activity—meaning it was intense enough to make them sweat and breathe hard for at least 20 minutes—three or more days in the week preceding the survey; only 20 percent participated in moderate physical activity such as walking or riding a bicycle for at least 30 minutes on five or more days of the previous week. More recently a 1998 study involving 302 students from the University of Pittsburgh found that only 39 percent of undergraduates reported exercising at any intensity three or more times per week, whereas 12 percent of students admitted they didn't exercise at all. Some researchers speculate that physical activity may be low among college students because of the amount of studying they do.

Are Unhealthy Eating Habits Contagious?

Since college students are generally on their own for the first time when it comes to food, maintaining a healthy weight can be enormously challenging as they adjust to campus life. Many gain weight and then begin to diet—either solo or with friends. And with more and more girls starting to diet in their early teens, they're experienced dieters by the time they enter college, and many are all too willing to share their personal strategies. A recent survey found that 91 percent of women on a college campus had tried to control their weight through dieting, whereas 22 percent were regular dieters.

Being preoccupied with body-image issues and dieting behaviors is often a collective concern among college women, and they frequently fuel these concerns in each other. What's more, going on fad diets together can even become a social thing or a bonding experience in the college years. "I remember people limiting their food choices in funny ways to try to lose weight," recalls Jenny, 36, a copywriter in northern California. "A lot of people ate nothing but bagels, and I remember a couple of women eating corn nuts obsessively instead of meals or less virtuous snacks. The women in my sorority were often competitive about how little they ate—at dinner, they'd brag that they hadn't eaten anything since breakfast. And since we ate family style and everybody was served the same food, everyone paid attention to how much everyone else was eating."

Such intense scrutiny combined with erratic eating habits can often trigger eating problems in those who are susceptible to them. Approximately 5 to 10 percent of American women are struggling with eating disorders, according to an organization called Eating Disorders Awareness and Prevention—and college women are no exception. But the most common eating problem on college campuses appears to be binge eating, also known as compulsive overeating, which, by some estimates, may affect as many as 30 percent of students. In a 1995 study, researchers at Loyola University in Chicago found that college women who were prone to bingeing tended to be more depressed and self-conscious and to have lower self-esteem, as well as more chaotic and extreme eating patterns, as their peers who didn't binge.

On some campuses, it appears that the Greek system may also contribute to unhealthy eating habits. In a 1997 study from the University of Maryland, researchers surveyed 625 members of a sorority and found that sorority sisters seem to have a greater fear of becoming fat; they're also more dissatisfied with their bodies and more preoccupied with weight and dieting than other college women from previous studies. The researchers concluded that sorority members are a subgroup that may be at increased risk for developing eating-related problems. What's more, a 1988 study from Yale University found that binge eating seemed to be contagious in the sorority environment: "In one sorority, the more one binged, the more popular one was," the author concluded. "By the end of the academic year, a sorority member's binge eating could be predicted from the binge-eating level of her friends." In this milieu, at least, it seems that binge eating may be a learned behavior that's spurred by social pressure.

College administrators around the country are becoming wise to the problem, and many schools now offer counseling programs that are designed to prevent or deal with eating disorders. So help is available, and best of all, it's often confidential. Because college students can be reluctant to participate in such programs because they feel ashamed or because they're worried about the stigma that's attached, many services now guarantee that such information won't be passed on to students' parents or to college administrators without their permission. Which means it's no longer risky to tell a counselor what's going on. Professionals aren't interested in policing students' eating behavior. They're simply there to help students loosen the emotional grip that eating disorders have on their sufferers—and avoid the devastating health consequences they can bring with them.

Students who work part-time—to help pay for tuition, room, board, or other expenses—may be at a further disadvantage. Between their class schedules, studying, and hours spent on the job, they may be perpetually strapped for free time. In which case, exercising may feel like a luxury compared to necessities like reading for class, writing papers, preparing for exams, or even sleeping.

And yet, by not exercising, college students are only short-changing themselves of a natural way to lose weight, sleep better, and decrease their risks of cancer, heart disease, diabetes, and other life-altering ailments. Plus, they're cheating themselves of one of the best stress busters around. Not only has research found that exercise relieves symptoms of depression and anxiety, but a series of studies at California State University, Long Beach, concluded that exercise appears to be the most effective mood-regulating behavior—better than listening to soothing music, venting your feelings to a friend, or eating comfort food.

The Party Life

Without a doubt, one of the most frequently overlooked sources of additional calories during college is alcohol, and if it's imbibed in great quantities, it can quickly contribute to weight gain. It's no secret that drinking is a popular pastime on college campuses; it's often a social activity, pure and simple. Research has found that students spend $4.2 billion a year on alcohol, and alcohol abuse seems to be becoming more widespread in college. In 1995, 35 percent of college students were episodic heavy drinkers (defined as having five or more drinks on one occasion), a significant increase from 1989, according to the National College Health Risk Behavior Survey.

Besides the extra calories consumed from beer, wine, or hard liquor, drinking can also lead students to eat more—whether it's by mindlessly munching on chips or popcorn at a party or while hanging out with friends. Then there's the post-party ritual of going out for a late-night snack or an early-morning meal as you swap stories about the evening's events. Similarly, getting high on marijuana—14 percent of students had done so in the 30 days preceding the 1995 National College Health Risk Behavior Survey—can leave students with a case of the munchies, an almost irresistible desire to snack. Indulged too often, these urges also can wreak havoc on a woman's efforts at weight control.

"I think I had too good a time in college," confesses Maria, 26, an executive assistant in Atlanta who added 20 pounds to her 5'2" frame during college. "It wasn't like I was eating because I was worried about grades or because I was lonely. I was having too much fun. A lot of the people I hung out with didn't worry about their weight, and eating became a real social thing for us. I lived in a sorority my sophomore year, and a group of us would make our own dinners, usually pasta and bread, and we'd often order pizza late at night while we were hanging out.

"But the drinking is what really contributed to my weight gain," she says. "I'd drink alcohol, mostly beer, three or four times a week, and I'm guessing I'd have eight beers on a given night. On the weekends, we'd go out and get a little drunk, then we'd go home and order pizza or cheese fries or we'd go to the diner and order turkey clubs or omelets, toast, and hash browns. The combination of eating more food and drinking really made me gain weight."

Dealing with Emotional Overload

For many people, college is often their first extended time away from home, not to mention their initial experience living on their own. And while this newfound independence can be exciting, it also brings a period of adjustment that can be unnerving, especially if you're suddenly far from everything that's familiar. So if students start feeling homesick or lonely, as they are bound to from time to time, it's easy to turn to favorite foods for comfort. Out of habit, they might start snacking on sugary or fat-laden treats, which are easily accessible even in dormitory life, in an effort to fill the emotional emptiness they're feeling.

Not only is eating a distracting activity, but it can be a way of numbing unpleasant emotions, such as loneliness, anxiety, or depression. For some people, it's often easier to deaden their negative feelings by eating than to tolerate them or articulate them. In a 1998 study of 580 college students, researchers from the Tokyo Institute of Psychiatry found that female students who had difficulty either identifying or describing their feelings were more likely to have abnormal eating habits or poor control over them.

Other people have a hard time differentiating between physical and emotional states of feeling—they find it difficult to tell the difference between anxiety and exhaustion, for example. As a result, they may head to the vending machine or the campus snack bar when they feel sad or stressed out or when they long for home because they're confusing emotional vulnerability with a physical need for food. In short, overeating becomes a way of handling emotions that are hard to decipher or reconcile. And while the desire to console and nurture yourself is a healthy instinct, turning to food to fulfill that desire isn't healthy because it can easily lead to weight gain.

"I remember visiting a friend from high school who went to college in New England and really wasn't happy her freshman year," recalls Anne, 25, an artist in San Francisco. "One afternoon, right after lunch, she and her roommate were sitting around, watching soap operas and complaining about how dismal their love lives were and how much they missed home. They started picking at a pecan pie her roommate's mother had sent, and before they knew it, they'd eaten the whole thing. Afterwards, they started calculating how many calories they'd each consumed—it turned out to be more than 1,500 calories apiece—but they didn't seem that worried about it. I got the feeling that this kind of emotional overeating wasn't unusual for them."

As with any stage of life, stress can also trigger the urge to nosh for some college students. Faced with keen academic competition or the rigors of taking exams or writing papers, some people may begin to eat out their frustrations. Similarly, relationship ups and downs and other disappointments can lead some college women—either solo or sometimes as a group—to drown their sorrows in favorite treats, be they gigantic bowls of popcorn, ice cream sundaes, or boxes of chocolates. Before long, this practice of eating to relieve emotions can become a habit. Not only can it backfire, making you feel worse after an eating binge, but this habit can become hard to break, too. The key is to find other, healthier ways to manage the day-to-day disappointments and frustrations of college life.

In addition, some women find themselves grappling with more biologically-based stressors. By some estimates, 50 to 75 percent of women experience some symptoms of premenstrual syndrome (PMS), which often worsens or occurs for the first time during periods of physical and psychological stress (such as college life). Some months probably are worse than others, and a woman's symptoms may be different from her friends' or roommates'—and that's quite normal. But an estimated 5 percent of women suffer such profound depression, rages, and other extreme symptoms in the late luteal phase (or second half) of the menstrual cycle that their ability to function screeches to a halt, a condition called premenstrual dysphoric disorder (PMDD).

To this day, the exact cause of PMS is poorly understood. Researchers suspect that premenstrual mood swings may stem from changes in the brain's chemistry that occur in response to monthly hormonal fluctuations. It may also be that PMS sufferers are simply more sensitive to these normal hormonal shifts. In either case, PMS is a very real condition—it's *not* all in your head—and it can affect your behavior, including how you think, feel, and eat.

Over the years, premenstrual food cravings—in particular, that undeniable penchant for cookies, chocolate, doughnuts, cake, or ice cream—have become the stuff of legends. In fact, research has found that women are particularly vulnerable to overeating during the premenstrual phase, which coincides with a time when levels of serotonin, the feel-good brain chemical, are naturally low. In a small 1989 study, researchers from the Massachusetts Institute of Technology found that women suffering from PMS significantly increased their calorie intake during the week before their period—from 1,892 calories to 2,395 calories per day. They also increased their consumption of carbohydrates—by 24 percent from meals and by 43 percent from snacks—which seemed to relieve their negative mood and boost their energy. The good news is, research has found that a woman's metabolic rate increases during the days before her period, so consuming slightly more calories than usual for a few days isn't likely to lead to lasting weight gain. But it will if PMS becomes an excuse to overeat all month long.

Fortunately, you can navigate your way through the premenstrual phase without losing complete control of your diet. Here are a few proven strategies to help ease PMS symptoms without compromising your waistline:

- **Tinker with your diet.** Eating smaller, more frequent meals—five or six spread throughout the day—and focusing on complex carbohydrate foods can help keep cravings in check. Cutting back on caffeine, alcohol, and salt can also help, especially during the seven to ten days before your period.

- **Increase your calcium intake.** A study from St. Luke's–Roosevelt Hospital Center in New York City found that when women who suffer from PMS took a total of 1,200 mg of calcium carbonate each day, they experienced nearly a 50 percent reduction in the severity of their symptoms—including mood swings, aches and pains, food cravings, and bloating—by the third cycle. Ideally, it's best to aim for a greater consumption of dairy products and calcium-rich foods, such as soy products, broccoli, and kale; if you just can't get enough calcium from food, check with your physician about taking a supplement.

- **Load up on carbohydrates.** Increasing your intake of breads, cereals, pasta, potatoes, and other starchy foods—which PMS sufferers often crave—may give your mood a lift without packing on unwanted pounds the way cake or cookies can. And there may be a physiological reason: These foods can trigger the release of serotonin.

- **Get moving.** You'd probably rather lie on the couch with a pint of Rocky Road, but you really should hit the trail or the treadmill. Regular aerobic exercise can alleviate many PMS symptoms as well as help women feel like they can cope better. Try to walk, jog, swim, or ride a bicycle for 30 minutes a day, stepping up your activity levels one to two weeks before your period is due.

- **Quiet your mind and body.** Even if you're skeptical about relaxation techniques such as yoga, guided imagery, and progressive muscle relaxation (consciously relaxing each major muscle group from your feet to your head—or vice versa), you may want to give them a try. Experts say they can all ease PMS symptoms and your response to stress. Rubbing your feet the right way can help, too. A study of 35 PMS sufferers, published in *Obstetrics & Gynecology,* found that reflexology—applying manual pressure to specific points on the hands or feet—significantly decreased their symptoms.

- **Consider medication.** If PMS is really interfering with your life and your ability to function, you may want to talk to a doctor about whether you're a good candidate for taking antidepressants. In recent years, SSRI antidepressants, such as Prozac, Paxil, and Zoloft, have been shown to help women with severe PMS.

Getting Through College Without Gaining Weight

When it comes to controlling your weight, awareness of your behavior is half the battle. After all, gaining weight during college isn't inevitable, especially now that you know the factors that can make you susceptible to packing on unwanted pounds. Your best bet is to come up with a game plan for avoiding these traps—by thinking about the choices you make for your meals, planning ahead to fit exercise into your life, and finding other outlets for stress and frustration. Here's how:

1. Eat regularly.

That means don't skip meals—and, most important, try to become a member of the breakfast club. People who eat a substantial breakfast, as well as lunch and dinner, burn 5 percent more calories per day than those who forgo the morning meal, according to researchers at the George Washington University School of Medicine. To keep your metabolism humming along efficiently, some diet experts recommend eating *at least* one-quarter of the day's calories at each meal—and making up the rest with healthy snacks.

By consuming meals at regular intervals throughout the day, you'll be supplied with plenty of continuous energy, and you'll be less likely to overeat than if you fuel up erratically. In the year after she graduated, Wendy, the New York writer, lost all the weight she'd gained during college, primarily by eating three square meals, including breakfast, every day. "I didn't even go on a diet," she says. "I just started eating more regularly and working out several times a week—and I've kept up these habits. If anything, I feel like I eat more now than when I was in college but I weigh 20 pounds less. My body's in a lot better shape now than when I was 19."

2. Make smart food selections.

Even though you've practically got a smorgasbord of offerings from which to choose your meals, try to hit all the major food groups at most meals while also keeping an eye on your fat intake. Most important, focus on getting the nutrients you need: at least 50 percent of the day's calories from carbohydrates, 15 percent from protein, and less than 30 percent from fat. Tracking the nutrients in your diet is a snap now that packaged foods are required to bear labels that contain specific nutritional information, including the fat, protein, and carbohydrate content. Also try to include three to five servings of vegetables and two to four servings of fruit per day.

Granted, it's often hard to know what ingredients are used in a complicated dish that's prepared by a food service, so you may be better off making simple selections—choosing broiled chicken (remove the skin yourself), green beans, and a baked potato for dinner over the Mexican casserole, for instance; having a turkey sandwich on whole-grain bread with lettuce, tomato, and sprouts for lunch instead of a slice of greasy pizza; or eating a bowl of high-fiber cereal topped with fresh fruit rather than a muffin or a Danish for breakfast. Many college dining halls also have salad bars that offer plenty of healthy selections—as long as you don't drown your creation in fat-filled salad dressing; choose low-fat versions, if available, or consider buying and bringing your own bottle.

It's also wise to plan ahead for snacks and late-night food cravings. If you keep items such as fresh or dried fruit, containers of low-fat ready-made pudding, small bags of pretzels, individual boxes of dry cereal, packages of sugar-free cocoa mix, or cups of soup on hand in your room, you'll be less likely to run for the vending machine or the phone when hunger strikes.

3. Follow the adage "All things in moderation."

For the sake of your figure, this should apply to consuming favorite high-fat foods as well as drinking alcohol. There's nothing wrong with eating ice cream or pizza late at night with friends— occasionally. If done regularly, however, you're likely to find unwanted pounds creeping onto your physique. A better idea is to make healthy choices most of the time, then to reward yourself once or twice a week or on the weekend. By the same token, try to limit your drinking to moderate amounts—and avoid binge drinking, which can hamper your judgment and coordination as well as your weight-control efforts.

4. Schedule exercise.

Since your class schedule is more or less fixed, you probably work in studying time around it. Why not do the same with exercise? If late afternoons are typically free, squeeze in a workout before dinner; likewise, if you have a break from midmorning until lunchtime, that's a good window of opportunity to hit the gym or fit in an aerobics class. The point is, you've got to think ahead about exercising rather than winging it; otherwise, your workouts will be hit-or-miss at best.

To improve your health and manage your weight, aim for at least 30 minutes of physical activity, most (preferably all) days of the week, and you'll fulfill the U.S. Surgeon General's basic exercise recommendation. To make exercise more fun—and boost your odds of making it a habit—find a workout buddy, sign up for a group class, or participate in a team sport (consider the intramural level if competitive sports don't appeal to you).

5. Cultivate new emotional outlets.

For those times when you do feel nostalgic for the old home life or you feel lonely in your new environment, it's smart to have an arsenal of healthy ways to nurture yourself at your disposal. Think about the types of activities that you enjoy and what's feasible in the college setting. If you live in a dormitory, you probably can't treat yourself to a bubble bath, but you could give yourself a manicure, buy yourself a new perfume, or cheer yourself up with a bouquet of flowers.

You could also start a journal or diary, which could be a boon to your physical and emotional well-being as you continue to adjust to college life. In a study at Southern Methodist University, researchers found that students who wrote about their intimate feelings about entering college, rather than superficial subjects, for 20 minutes per day, three days per week, had significantly fewer visits to the health center for physical illnesses over the next several months. Not only does writing about emotionally charged experiences stimulate an increase in the activity of the body's immune system, but researchers believe that translating emotional experiences into language helps to organize them so that you understand them better. This, in turn, helps you stop dwelling on your feelings, which can eliminate the urge to nosh for emotional reasons.

6. Make new friends.

Be careful: Some people in your life may, intentionally or not, sabotage your weight-control efforts by pushing food, encouraging you to order a sub sandwich late at night "just this once," or by saying things like "It's just too hard to watch what you eat here." Others may simply elicit the behavior you're trying to avoid. If you generally overindulge when you go out with a certain group of friends, you may need to stop hanging out with them for a while or find something else to do with them instead. For example, if you often go out for ice cream with certain pals, you might try to arrange a date with them at the gym or make a plan to go for a hike as an alternative. The key is to find allies who can support the habits you're trying to establish.

For Better or Worse,
For Thinner or Heavier

Though Katie had been unhappy with her weight in high school, that was nothing compared to what happened shortly after her wedding in 1987. "I married a thin man who can eat whatever he wants without gaining weight, and I started eating the way he

eats," explains Katie, 35, an engineer from the Milwaukee area. "We would go out to eat late at night or we'd go to happy hour. He came from a family that liked fried food, so I started frying food that I thought he would like. And wherever we were, I would eat the same size portions he did. My metabolism couldn't handle it, and I gained 45 pounds in the first year and a half of marriage."

As the years passed, and after being pregnant with each of her two children, Katie gained even more weight, until the scale finally registered 90 pounds more than her premarital weight. "I'd heard that people often put on weight during their first year of marriage, but I didn't think about it happening to me," Katie says. "I ignored the scale for a long time. It was a shock when I finally stepped on it."

There's no question: Getting married ranks up there among life's most significant and rewarding acts. It plays an enormous role in the lives of most people, considering that approximately 90 percent of people in the United States marry eventually. But the months leading up to and following your declarations of everlasting love can be tumultuous, to say the least. From the moment the question is popped, you're on a wild, wonderful rollercoaster, from the engagement to the big event and into the honeymoon. After that, the real adjustment begins—to living as a "we" instead of an "I," to creating a home that you share, to starting a family perhaps. But one of the things no one tells most brides is that tying the knot can lead them to gain weight. Indeed, many brides can no longer fit into their wedding dresses by their fifth anniversary.

Granted, men also gain weight after marrying, but they appear to do so more gradually. In a 1995 study, researchers at Cornell University surveyed more than 2,400 adults about how their weight fluctuated in relation to changes in marital status. What they found is that women tend to experience more immediate shifts than men do. Women who became married gained an average of five pounds over one year; men who got married, in contrast, experienced no significant weight change over the newlywed period.

These patterns seem to change with the passing years, however. In a national study involving nearly 5,000 adults, researchers from the Centers for Disease Control and Prevention (CDC) found that both men and women who were married gained weight over a ten-year period. While the men gained an average of nearly half a point in their body mass index (BMI), women who walked down the aisle gained nearly a whole point in BMI. In another study, researchers from the CDC found that women who became married were 50 percent more likely to experience major weight gain (defined as an increase of 13 kilograms—the equivalent of 28.6 pounds—or more) over a decade than those who were already married and remained so. Meanwhile, when researchers placed a questionnaire in a national magazine aimed at weight-conscious women, 9,000 women responded. On average, women who had been married 13 years gained 24.7 pounds, while their husbands put on 19.4 pounds.

Other studies have found that advancing age, job status, and childbearing have as much of an effect on a woman's weight as her conjugal status. It could also be that some women don't gain as much weight after marrying partly because society values appearance and thinness more highly for women than for men, regardless of whether they're single or married. Researchers have speculated that women who don't gain weight after marrying may be making more of an effort to control their weight because they're more motivated by these societal standards than men are.

Togetherness and Weight

How can getting married influence your weight? Let us count the ways. First of all, when you get married, you not only share a home but a refrigerator and a pantry, too. And women may find themselves eating what their husbands typically eat, which may be heavier food, more snack foods, or larger quantities. While single, many women tend to eat simple meals, especially for dinner; once they marry, by contrast, they may be having more complete meals, consisting of multiple offerings. And since many women assume the responsibility for food shopping, meal planning, and cooking, they often wind up spending more time thinking about food and handling it in the kitchen, which can encourage them to eat more. In fact, a 1999 study by researchers at the University of Minnesota School of Public Health found that, by and large, men aren't spending much time in the kitchen these days. Just 23 percent of married men are involved in meal planning, compared to 93 percent of women; 36 percent of men do at least some of the grocery shopping, whereas 88 percent of

How Splitting Up Affects a Woman's Weight

It's one of those things that can go either way. If a woman gets divorced and suddenly feels sad, bored, or lonely, she might be likely to gain weight if she begins overeating for emotional reasons, such as craving companionship or feeling overburdened as a single parent. But if divorce is a blessing in her eyes—perhaps because it frees her from the tyranny of an unhappy marriage or because she's looking forward to getting a fresh, independent start—she may end up losing weight. After all, she may begin to eat lighter meals now that she's cooking for one again, or she may become more figure-conscious because she'll be re-entering the singles scene.

In 1997, Patricia, 28, an interior designer who lives outside San Francisco, got divorced after ten years of marriage. During the last two years of her marriage, she'd gained 20 pounds after relocating, and the weight remained on her frame. It wasn't until after her husband moved out of their home that she made an effort to lose weight. "When he left, I started dieting and exercising regularly and I began reading about nutrition and exercise," women do; and 27 percent of men do some meal preparation, compared with 90 percent of women.

As a couple, you also may be having a glass of wine with dinner every night or going out to eat more frequently than you used to, which can make your calorie intake creep up. In fact, when researchers at the University of Memphis examined the daily diet records of 129 premenopausal women, they found that those who ate out at restaurants frequently—between 6 and 13 times during the week—consumed more calories (288 more, to be exact), as well as more fat and sodium, per day than those who consumed most of their meals at home. Ingesting nearly 300 more calories per day, the researchers concluded, "might lead to a steady increase in weight."

she explains. "I felt very uncomfortable—I was too fat at that weight. I decided to lose weight to make myself feel better. And I was starting to feel lonely, so I wanted to make myself attractive to other people." Within a short time, she'd lost the 20 pounds she'd gained, plus 10 more. "Now I feel more attractive," she says, "and my clothes fit much better."

Patricia is hardly the only woman to lose weight after splitting with her spouse. Indeed, in a 1995 study involving more than 2,400 adults, researchers at Cornell University found that women who got divorced lost an average of nearly 3 pounds over a year—without even trying. Similarly, a 1992 study from the University of Texas found that men and women whose status changed from married to unmarried had lower body mass indexes after three years than those who remained married. The weight loss may be due to changes in eating habits that result from the loss of one's regular dining companion—or to the release of stress after dissolving an unhappy marriage. Either way, it appears that many women shed pounds along with their marital misery.

Granted, it's hard to monitor your calorie intake when you're dining out often because it's impossible to actually know what's in the food you're eating unless you prepare it. Even experts have a hard time estimating fat and calorie content at restaurants. In a survey conducted by the Center for Science in the Public Interest and researchers at New York University, professionally trained dietitians underestimated the fat content of five restaurant meals by an average of 49 percent; they misjudged the calorie content by an average of 37 percent. Clearly, dining out loosens the control you have over your calorie intake.

Moreover, many people become less physically active after they marry. This may be partly because life as a couple—between your social schedule and your commitments to your respective families—keeps you busier than ever. But it could also be a result of the fact that many couples would rather spend free time relaxing with each other—or cocooning in their new home—than exercising. After all, it's much harder to force yourself to roll out of bed and go for an early morning jog when your loved one is lying beside you. Similarly, heading to the gym after work becomes a lot less appealing when your honey is waiting for you at home. And if the couple has an active social life, that puts another time constraint on their ability to exercise. So much of marriage-related weight gain seems to involve lifestyle changes.

But a woman's mindset, particularly how much of her self-image revolves around her appearance, can also influence whether or not she gains weight after her nuptials. While single, women, in particular, often make more of an effort to keep themselves slim and attractive; whether they admit it to themselves or not, being attractive in the eyes of men is often a large concern for those in the singles world. But after you've said your "I do's"—and you've removed yourself from romantic circulation—that concern is no longer as paramount, which means that you might gradually relax the strict eating and exercise standards you've imposed on yourself, a change many women relish after years of self-denial. It also means that you might let down your guard when it comes to controlling your weight.

After all, when you feel loved, sexy, and secure in your relationship, the extra padding that's beginning to appear on your hips and thighs or the love handles that are developing around your midsection may not seem like a big deal. You might figure that if it doesn't bother him, why should it bother you? While it's healthy and very grown-up to pay more attention to the quality of your married life than the circumference of your thighs, relaxing your dietary vigilance too much could cause the number on the scale to creep slowly but steadily upward. Not only can this affect how a woman feels about her body, but gaining an excessive amount of weight can affect her health—both in the short term (setting her up for back problems, varicose veins, and fatigue, among other discomforts) and in the long run (increasing her risk of heart disease, hypertension, diabetes, and certain forms of cancer, among other conditions). Which means that if she's not careful, she may not be around to celebrate her 50th wedding anniversary.

Another factor often influencing a married woman's weight is the role she assumes in the household. From childhood through adulthood, food, nurturing, and security are often inextricably linked: For many women, feeling loved is often associated with memories of growing up in a household where Mom baked cookies and lovingly prepared meals for the whole family; once they marry, some women want to re-create that tradition of preparing or providing special, comforting foods as a way of showing love to their husbands. While this desire is well intended, it can lead a woman to snack more as she spends increasing amounts of time around food. Moreover, when a woman takes on the jobs of creating a home and assuming complete responsibility for food shopping, meal planning, and cooking, such an emphasis on food-related tasks can cause her to eat more throughout the day—nibbling while shopping or tending to a pot on the stove, for example—often without her realizing it. Meanwhile, for women

The Health Benefits of Marriage

Study after study has found that married people tend to live longer and more healthfully than single people do. And the beneficial effects seem to be more pronounced for men than for women. Research has found, for example, that married men are more likely to protect their health by engaging in behaviors such as getting enough sleep, avoiding dangerous risks, and steering clear of substance abuse. What's more, women who get married often decrease their alcohol intake, according to research involving more than 6,000 people at the University of Texas in Austin. (By contrast, this study found that getting divorced is associated with an increase in negative health behavior, such as greater tobacco use and alcohol consumption.)

Part of this effect undoubtedly stems from the fact that women are socialized not only to safeguard their own health but to be nurturing and heedful to the needs of others. So if a woman assumes this role in her marriage, she's more likely to monitor her spouse's health and behavior, which can help improve his well-being. In other words, she becomes the keeper of the family's health. "Since I got married in 1989, I've been eating a lot more healthfully," says Jon, 35, a lawyer from New York City. "I never used to think about eating fruits and vegetables; I'd just grab a sandwich or greasy fast food on the run. In the first two years of our marriage, my cholesterol dropped 75 points and my good cholesterol went up. And it's because my wife helped me change my eating habits."

In addition, mortality rates and the risk of overall disease tend to be lower for married people than for single people. Here, too, marriage seems to be more beneficial for men than women, although women do reap health advantages. What's the link? One of the primary theories is that these benefits stem from the support and sense of connection one derives from living with a spouse; this loving, bolstering relationship appears to provide a buffer to stress and negative emotions (such as loneliness or depression), as well as their harmful effects on the body.

with demanding jobs outside the home, the added responsibilities brought on by becoming a wife as well as organizing and running a household can lead some women to eat for emotional reasons, which can gradually lead to weight gain.

When Happily Ever After Doesn't Happen

Wedded bliss—it's the stuff of fairy tales and daydreams dating back to girlhood. But in those marriages in which the promise doesn't become a reality, the sense of disappointment can be crushing. Indeed, for some women, the primary source of weight gain stems from their frustration over the loss of excitement from their courtship days, from continuous marital spats, or from feeling generally unhappy with the state of married life. Particularly if anger toward their husband enters the equation, many women try to swallow these unpleasant feelings with food. After all, we've been raised to believe that getting angry isn't socially acceptable for women; as a result, many of us try to suppress these feelings—or turn to favorite foods to help calm the rage. Other times, women can end up overeating to cope with the emotional void, disappointment, or loneliness they feel when their hopes of living happily ever after have been dashed. Food, especially favorite treats, ends up becoming a substitute for the love and affection they're not getting from their spouses.

If anyone knows this, it's Ann, 39, a mother of five children who does part-time farm work near Vancouver. In the 22 years of her marriage, her weight has gone up and down like a yo-yo, varying with the quality of her relationship with her husband. "I got married at age 17 to an older man, and neither one of us was prepared for marriage," explains Ann, whose weight has fluctuated by nearly 75 pounds in the ensuing years. "We had too many expectations of each other, but we weren't letting each other know what they were. We just weren't communicating. So I felt very lonely even in a house full of people. You figure when you get married that you're not going to feel alone anymore, but it happens."

Before long, Ann's eating habits became erratic as she tried to deal with her mounting disappointments. "When our marriage started going downhill, I wouldn't eat for most of the day, and then I would get so hungry that I would eat whatever was there, whether it was healthy or not," she recalls. "When I felt really frustrated, I'd do something to distract myself, like clean the house from top to bottom, then I'd get so hungry that I'd eat goodies like doughnuts, cake, or cookies. Sometimes I'd buy a box of 12 doughnuts and I'd finish them off by the end of the day. During one problem-filled time, I ate a whole gallon of ice cream one night. Sometimes I'd prepare meals and my husband wouldn't show up, so I'd eat his portion and mine. I think I was eating more and drinking more alcohol to fill an emptiness I felt inside. Alcoholism runs in my family, and I realized that drinking wasn't healthy, so I stopped. But I think I may have transferred that addiction to food."

Ann was on the verge of leaving her husband when he finally agreed to try to become more emotionally available. The two made a pact to be more honest with each other, and he became more supportive through family crises. Gradually their marriage improved and so did Ann's eating habits. "The whole family is eating more healthfully now; it's become a lifestyle choice," she says. "I eat more regularly now—three meals and two small snacks each day—and I don't binge like I used to." As a result, Ann has lost 25 pounds.

Meanwhile, other women use their excess weight as an excuse to prevent them from acting on their sexual desires. For these women, consciously or not, their extra body fat acts as a barrier to intimacy with their husbands; at the same time, it also removes the temptation to have an affair because they don't feel attractive enough to consider the possibility. This is particularly effective in our culture because obesity is often viewed as a physical turn-off. Indeed, several studies have found that many obese people use overeating as a way to avoid sexual relationships or unwanted sexual attention. In the survey of 9,000 women, for example, 75 percent of the respondents said that weight gain made them feel less comfortable about being naked. But the relationship between eating and intimacy can often spiral out of control. Many women wind up overeating in an attempt to relieve sexual frustration, but this only adds pounds and creates more of a barrier to sexual contact, which, in turn, can increase sexual frustration, and so on.

And if a man begins to nag or denigrate his wife about her extra girth, this simply adds fuel to the fire. It might increase the resentment she feels toward him or cause her to rebel against his wishes by gaining more weight. Although this allows her to escape his efforts to control her, she ends up harming herself. Her body becomes a battleground, and her weight becomes a weapon to use against him—but it often backfires, hurting her instead. Unfortunately, in this scenario, no one emerges as the victor.

Resetting the Table

Complicating the issue of marriage and weight is the fact that in some marriages, one person's desire to lose weight—usually the woman's—is often seen as a disruption of the status quo. Eating and having a table set for two may have become such an integral part of a couple's life together that the husband may view any attempts on his wife's part to lose weight as a rejection of the life he's grown accustomed to. He may be resistant to changing his own eating patterns. Or he may be unwilling to do something about his own weight problem and may resent her for trying to tackle hers. As a result, he may wind up sabotaging her efforts to shed pounds—sometimes intentionally but more often not. On some level, he may fear that if she slims down and becomes more attractive, his wife will leave him or have an affair. Or he might be afraid that he'll lose the upper hand in their relationship if her self-confidence soars after she loses weight. Instead of confronting these issues head on, he uses subversive tactics to keep his wife heavy.

In their book *Weight, Sex & Marriage,* Richard Stuart, a former psychological director of Weight Watchers International, and Barbara Jacobson describe the many ways in which husbands often undermine their wives' weight-reduction efforts in a desire to restore or maintain a sense of equilibrium in the relationship. In some instances, a man might send his wife mixed messages about losing weight. On the surface, he may encourage her to slim down, but then he ends up complaining when she prepares low-calorie meals for the family or he gripes about the high cost

How Exercise Affects Your Sex Life

The debate about whether exercise makes a person sexier has been raging for decades. And while there's still no definitive answer to this titillating question, there is some evidence that regular, moderate exercise can, indeed, improve a person's sex life by enhancing libido and sexual satisfaction.

In one study, researchers at Chicago State University surveyed 500 women, ages 18 to 45, who participated regularly in aerobic dance, calisthenics, or weight-training classes, and found that nearly 60 percent reported greater satisfaction with their "sexual selves" since they started their exercise program. What's more, nearly 25 percent of the women reported experiencing spontaneous orgasm or sexual arousal *while* exercising, and almost 30 percent experienced an increase in libido immediately after working out.

In a 1996 study at the University of Washington School of Medicine, researchers had 36 women watch an ordinary film or an erotic film in two different sessions; before one of the sessions, the women exercised intensely for 20 minutes. It turned out that after exercising, the women were more aroused by the erotic film.

of joining a health club. Other forms of sabotage are more overt—such as demanding that she prepare high-calorie meals he knows she can't resist, bringing home a box of chocolates or insisting on taking her out to a restaurant that serves rich food as a reward for losing weight, offering to do the grocery shopping and purchasing lots of items she's trying to avoid, or complaining about being lonely when she goes out to exercise.

But many men end up thwarting their wives' weight-loss efforts without meaning to. They don't intend any harm. These men are simply out of touch with what's helpful and what's not when a spouse is trying to shed unwanted pounds. Or they may

Specifically, they experienced greater vaginal blood flow and responsiveness. Meanwhile, research at the Center for Marital and Sexual Studies in Long Beach, California, has found that exercisers have easier orgasms than those who are not physically fit.

It's not clear whether these benefits stem from the physiological effects of exercise—increased circulation, the release of endorphins, improved muscle tone, or enhanced overall health, among others—or from the mood-elevating aspects of exercise, or from improvements in body image and self-esteem that people typically experience after starting to exercise regularly. There could even be a cumulative effect among these factors. (Excessive exercise, by contrast, appears to dampen sex drive in men, possibly by disrupting the balance of hormones, but that's not a concern for most people.)

Whatever the underlying mechanism(s) may be, the promise of a more sizzling sex life is yet another reason to get moving. To enhance the level of sexuality and passion in your marriage, you and your spouse should aim to exercise for 30 to 45 minutes at a moderate intensity at least three days per week. In all likelihood, you'll both be glad you did.

not realize how much they can influence their wives' eating habits. In these instances, it's up to you to help your husband become your ally by giving him concrete suggestions on what he

The Benefits of Your Spouse's Support

There's no doubt about it: When your spouse supports your commitments to exercise and improve your eating habits, these goals become that much easier to attain. Indeed, research has found that getting support, especially from the home front, plays a pivotal role in helping people develop habits that can help them lose weight and maintain their weight loss. For example, a 1995 study from Indiana University found that adults who joined an exercise program with their spouses were much more likely to stick with it than were those who joined on their own; after a year, 94 percent of married couples were still going strong, whereas only 57 percent of the solo exercisers were still participating in the fitness program.

Meanwhile, other studies show that a spouse's support and involvement in his partner's efforts to alter her eating habits or weight-control efforts play a critical role in determining success. A 1995 study from Israel, for example, concluded that "perceived spouse support predicted continual involvement" for 42 overweight women in a community-based weight-control program. Moreover, a 1999 study from the University of Pittsburgh School of Medicine found that social support—on the part of friends or family members—helped participants not only complete a weight-loss treatment but maintain their weight loss 10 months later. And in a study from the University of Manitoba in Canada, researchers found that women whose spouses were trained in modeling, monitoring, and reinforcing weight-loss techniques lost significantly more weight can say or do to support the changes you're trying to make. It may also help to reassure him that you won't love him any less if you lose weight, just because there's less of you.

after 3, 6, and 12 months than those whose spouses didn't cooperate; interestingly, the researchers concluded that "instructing spouses not to sabotage their wives' efforts may be as effective for long-term maintenance as actively training them to aid their wives."

How can you make the most of this built-in support system? Your best bet is to discuss your plans to lose weight with your husband, then to ask for the kind of help you want. Think of it as coaching your husband on how he can best help you. You probably don't want him to police what you're eating, for example, but he could help you by offering encouragement or motivation when you most need it, by helping you track your progress and cheering you along the way, by acting as your exercise buddy when other plans fall through, or simply by not bringing home tempting foods you want to avoid. He could also eat the same foods that you're eating on your weight-loss plan but in larger quantities; or he could take over some of the food preparation chores so that you can spend less time thinking about food in general.

Above all, be direct and specific in letting him know what he can say or do that will be most beneficial to you. Don't expect him to read your mind—it's not fair, and it won't give you the assistance you need. Once he's begun to give you the kind of support you depend on, acknowledge, thank, and reward him to ensure that it continues. There's nothing like positive reinforcement to inspire him to keep up the good work.

Living As a Couple
Without Gaining Weight

Maybe nobody warned you about the hazards of gaining weight when you walked down the aisle. But now you know how getting married can lead you to lose control of your weight. Avoiding these diet and lifestyle traps isn't going to be a breeze; it's going to take some effort and, most of all, mindfulness about your eating and exercise habits. But it is possible to remain happily married and still fit into your wedding dress on your tenth anniversary. Here's how:

1. **Pay attention to portion sizes.**

One of the keys to preventing marriage-related weight gain is to be aware of just how much *you're* eating. After all, eating can be social, and when you're cooking with a man, it's easier to eat more—while you're cooking, during the meal, or while you're putting away the leftovers. Your best bet is to continuously compare what you're eating overall to what you typically ate before you were married; if it's more,

then you need to pare back. By the same token, pay attention to *when* you eat. If your husband has a habit of munching on chips or another form of junk food while watching a ballgame on TV, you don't need to join him; instead, you could keep him company without noshing.

To help you become aware of how your eating habits have changed with your wedded status, keep track of what you eat and when you eat it in a food diary. This way, you'll become more conscious of your behavior, which can either help you stop eating when you don't want to be or figure out how to replace snacking with a healthier behavior (such as knitting while watching TV together). In a 1998 study at the Center for Behavioral Medicine in Chicago, researchers found that keeping a food diary not only helped the nearly 40 participants control their weight during high-risk holidays but even helped them shed unwanted pounds. A related follow-up study found that even if people don't keep track of their behavior every single day, doing so 75 percent of the time was enough to help them kiss bad eating habits good-bye.

2. Exercise together.

Or try to arrange to work out at the same time if you're concerned about missing out on time together. These strategies actually serve two purposes: They take away the guilt from being unavailable for your spouse, and they can reinforce your commitment to exercise regularly because you're doing it together (or simultaneously), which can make you feel accountable for your exercise habits. Similarly, including more physical activity for two—a bike ride, playing tennis or golf, and so on—in your weekends can increase the amount of movement and togetherness in your life.

3. Make smart choices when dining out.

If you're seriously watching your fat or calorie intake, it helps to plan ahead what type of item you might order and try not to go to the restaurant famished; otherwise, you'll only be likely to overeat. Once you're there, act as your own food sleuth by asking questions about how dishes are prepared. In general, you're better off ordering something baked, broiled, grilled, steamed, roasted, or boiled. You can also ask to have a dish prepared without added fat. A recent survey by the National Restaurant Association found that more than 94 percent of restaurants will alter their preparation methods if a customer requests it.

Whenever possible, select leaner cuts of meat, such as round steak, filet mignon, or center-cut pork or lamb chops. And remove the skin from poultry before eating it. Requesting sauce or salad dressing on the side is another way of conserving calories; that way, you can control how much goes on the food. Dip your fork into the sauce or dressing then stab a morsel of meat or several leaves of lettuce, and you'll get the flavor with every bite but much less fat and fewer calories than if the dish were slathered with the stuff.

Also, when dining out, don't feel compelled to match your husband course for course if he's one of those lucky people who can eat whatever he wants without adding pounds. Consider ordering two appetizers instead of one plus an entree—or sharing a dessert instead of having your own.

4. Shop wisely.

If you've assumed responsibility for food shopping, be sure to follow Rule Number One: Don't go to the grocery store when you're hungry. Wait until after a meal, then shop for food with a list in hand to maximize efficiency. Spend most of your time along the perimeter of the store, where the healthiest choices—such as produce, dairy, and the fish, poultry, and meat counters—are located. Also get in the habit of reading labels—they're full of helpful information, from fat content to nutrient values, as well as calorie counts.

5. Don't use food to fulfill emotional needs.

If there's something missing from your relationship—or if you're dealing with marital strife—eating to soothe yourself is only likely to come back to haunt you, making you feel more miserable as you gain weight. What's more, it won't solve your problems. You'd be wiser to try to address your marital troubles directly—either with each other or with the help of a counselor—and find other outlets for your frustration—such as exercising or playing with your dog—in the meantime.

6. Recognize that only you can control your eating habits.

It sounds so obvious, but many people forget this truism. It doesn't matter what your loved one says or does, you—and only you—are the one who controls what you eat and how much. Once you realize this, it becomes much less difficult to separate your eating habits from the complex issues that may have fueled overeating in your marriage. Plus, if you abide by this truth—and repeat it aloud, if need be—your spouse will likely come to accept it and stop pushing food or thwarting your weight-loss efforts. And that will make it so much easier for you to stay in the driver's seat when it comes to controlling your weight.

The Weight-Related Perils of Pregnancy

"When I was pregnant with all three of my children, I *really* ate," confesses Gwen, 36, a lawyer in the Philadelphia area who had struggled with her weight off and on since she was a teenager. "I knew I had an excuse not to be thin, so I gave myself license to eat

whatever I wanted. I ate huge portions of food, much more than I would normally eat—I could eat a whole pizza by myself while I was pregnant. With all three pregnancies, I was very nauseous for the first five months, so I just kept eating to try to alleviate the nausea—I felt better if I prevented my stomach from getting empty. I craved bread, pasta, Philly cheese steak, and cookies, so I would eat these instead of things that were good for me."

With each pregnancy, Gwen gained 35 to 43 pounds, and while she lost most of the weight afterward, she carried an extra 10 pounds from one pregnancy to the next. After giving birth to her third child in 1997, she found herself with 53 unwanted pounds on her 5'3" frame. "I felt and looked horrible," she recalls. "And I felt completely overwhelmed at the prospect of having to lose all that weight. I was envious of the people who'd only gained 20-some pounds and had less of a struggle to get it off."

There's no question that pregnancy is treacherous territory when it comes to weight control. It's a time when a variety of factors seem to conspire against a woman to make her loosen the reins on her eating habits. For starters, many women, like Gwen, adopt the attitude that they're eating for two, so they begin eating extra-large portions at meals and snacks whenever they feel like it. While it's true that an expectant mother is nourishing two heartbeats, the idea that she needs to eat twice as much as normal is actually a misconception because the baby's caloric needs are significantly lower than the mother's. But since this is one of the only times in a woman's life when she's actually *supposed to* gain weight, some women give in to this expectation with reckless abandon, figuring that if they're going to gain weight, it doesn't really matter how much they gain.

Indeed, research has found that even women who normally obsess about every bite they put in their mouths when they're not pregnant become less restrained in their eating habits during pregnancy. Of course, this attitude shift is liberating and healthy—to a point. And it may partly reflect the fact that with all the changes that are happening to her body, an expectant mother may feel entitled to eat whatever she wants, especially if she feels deprived because she's given up caffeine, alcohol, or cigarettes for the baby's sake.

In 1996, pregnant with her second child, Ginny, 36, a copywriter in northern California who is normally careful about what she eats, was in her fourth month when her eating habits veered off course. Though she'd been sticking with a balanced, nutritious diet, the Christmas holidays snuck up on her and derailed her self-control. "I had made Christmas cookies to take on our annual family ski trip, and I ate them all before we left on the trip," she recalls. "I was ravenous all the time, and I fell into this 'Oh, poor me' mentality. I felt that since I was pregnant and tired and I already had a toddler, I deserved to indulge myself. But I overdid it—at home and while we were visiting my family. I ate healthy meals, but I also snacked whenever I felt like it. I must have eaten an average of eight cookies a day for a month. I felt like I had a built-in excuse for bingeing, and I just kept going for a month."

Her wake-up call came at her next appointment with her obstetrician. In the month since her last checkup, she'd gained ten pounds. "I remember the midwife asked me what I'd been eating, and when I told her Christmas cookies, she said it was time for a little nutrition counseling," Ginny says. "After that, I ate much more healthfully. I'd had my sweet fling, and I realized that if I kept going like that, I'd gain too much weight."

Dealing with Your Changing Shape

During pregnancy, a woman also may struggle with body-image issues. After a lifetime spent scrutinizing the size and shape of her body, she may feel emotionally at odds with her growing girth and physically uncomfortable moving around. Which is hardly surprising, considering that we live in a society that prizes slim, svelte figures. Instead of viewing her burgeoning belly as a sign of beauty, as the ultimate symbol of fertility, an expectant mother might fret over just how large she seems to be getting. Moreover, she may fear that the slim, trim figure she's fought so hard to attain or maintain may be gone for good. When researchers from the University of California, San Francisco, interviewed 221 women about the most frequent causes of pregnancy stress, concerns about body image were second from the top of the list (physical discomfort was number one). These women used words like *fat*, *unattractive*, and *distorted* to describe their changing

The Food Whims of Pregnancy

It's become the stuff of legends: stories of expectant mothers who are overcome by middle-of-the-night pangs for ice cream, kosher dills, or double-stuffed tacos—or who become violently nauseated at the mere scent of fish or coffee at any time of day. The truth is, while pregnancy-related food cravings and aversions are common, they aren't usually this intense.

At least half of expectant mothers are likely to experience a craving for a particular food or to have at least one food aversion during the nine-month stretch. A 1994 study from Sri Lanka found that 47 percent of pregnant women had cravings for particular foods, whereas a 1992 study of pregnant adolescents, conducted by researchers at the University of Tennessee, found that 86 percent of expectant mothers had cravings and 66 percent experienced aversions to previously liked foods. But it's not always easy to tease out what's truly due to pregnancy and what's a normal food yearning or rejection, which we all have from time to time. There is at least some hormonal connection, though: Cravings and aversions do appear to be more common in the first trimester, when hormones fluctuate the most. Some women have a particular hankering for foods such as dairy products, citrus bodies, despite the fact that they were changing for a good reason—because there was new life inside.

Not only can feeling awkward in her own skin affect a woman's ability to enjoy her pregnancy, but it can trigger stress-related eating, which can lead to excessive weight gain. In other words, feeling upset that she can't control what's happening to her body can lead a mother-to-be to use food to comfort herself, which can lead to overeating. So can anxiety about what's to come. During the nine-month stint, there are bound to be times when a woman

fruits, and spicy dishes, whereas the smell of fish, meat, fried foods, coffee, and red meat can often kill a mom-to-be's appetite during these months.

Doctors rarely subscribe to the notion that a craving or an aversion is a sign from the body that it needs or should avoid a particular food. But that doesn't mean it's easy to ignore cravings and aversions, especially since there appears to be a psychological component. When an expectant mother is riding an emotional rollercoaster, especially in early pregnancy, fulfilling food cravings may represent a way of nurturing herself—or having someone else cater to her needs and desires. And there's nothing wrong with giving in and having a hot fudge sundae or a doughnut occasionally, so long as you stick to a balanced diet most of the time.

One craving that should never be indulged, however, is a condition called *pica*. This is characterized by an intense desire to eat such substances as clay, laundry starch, dirt, ashes, chalk, or cornstarch—things you wouldn't dream of eating normally. This yearning can be a sign of a nutritional deficiency, such as an iron deficiency, so it should be reported immediately to your doctor.

becomes preoccupied with, even uncertain about, the impending arrival of her little one. Nagging questions of *Will the baby be healthy? Will I be a good mother? Can I handle this responsibility? How will our lives change?* will undoubtedly surface now and again. In addition, she may worry about how having a child will affect her marriage, which isn't an idle concern, since research suggests that having a baby can be hard on a marriage in the first year of parenting. These worries also can spark bouts of emotional eating.

Aside from these emotional issues, a variety of physiological factors can cause even a healthy eater's diet to go haywire when she's pregnant. A mother-to-be's eating habits are often complicated by pregnancy-related symptoms, such as constant hunger, morning sickness (which can strike at any time of day), and heartburn, as well as food cravings and aversions (see "The Food Whims of Pregnancy" on page 66). Many women find that eating certain foods, especially proteins and carbohydrates, seems to quell queasiness and an insatiable appetite; so does eating frequent mini-meals throughout the day and snacking during the night to prevent the stomach from ever becoming truly empty. But if done to excess, this, too, can lead to excess weight gain.

When all these factors are considered together, it's no wonder most women tend to walk away from pregnancy with extra pounds. Research has found that the average lasting weight gain associated with childbearing is 2.2 pounds, but this varies widely, depending on the women studied and the timeframe in which their weight was checked. In studies that have examined a woman's weight gain from before pregnancy to 6 to 12 months after childbirth, for example, the average weight retention after pregnancy has ranged from 2 pounds to 8.4 pounds. Meanwhile, a 1996 study from the University of Texas in Austin found that women retained an average of 7.3 pounds 6 months after delivery and 5.1 pounds 18 months after delivery. In contrast, retrospective data on obese women has found that 73 percent gained 22 pounds or more in the year after childbirth.

These gains are significant because when women carry extra weight from one pregnancy to the start of the next, it can set them up for considerable weight gain over the years. And this, in turn, can increase their risks of myriad health problems, including heart disease, diabetes, and breast cancer. Moreover, research has found that the most powerful predictor of whether a woman gets her body back after having a baby is how much weight she gains during a particular pregnancy. Granted, many other variables come into play, as well. A woman's genetic and ethnic heritage has a strong influence (for example, research has found that during pregnancy black women tend to gain more weight than white women do; they also seem to retain more weight after the postpartum period). In addition, a woman's eating and exercise habits in the postpartum period, her stress level, and how soon she returns to work all can have an impact on how much weight she retains after pregnancy. But of all of these, the amount of weight gained during pregnancy appears to matter most.

The Right Way to Gain During Pregnancy

While many women relax their dietary vigilance during pregnancy—and even enjoy eating foods they wouldn't normally allow themselves to eat—the nine-month stretch shouldn't be seen as license to go hog wild. The average woman who isn't pregnant and isn't dieting needs to consume between 1,800 and 2,200 calories per day; during pregnancy, she'll need only an additional 300 calories each day to maintain good health and help the baby grow properly. That's not much. If she consumes three glasses of low-fat milk a day or has a whole-wheat bagel with cream cheese for a snack, she'll easily fulfill her body's additional calorie requirements. But if she reaches for handful after handful of cookies, candy, chips, or other high-fat treats, she'll quickly exceed those calorie requirements, setting herself up for excessive weight gain. Not only is it harder to lose afterward, but gaining too much weight during pregnancy carries its own health risks—including an increased risk of high blood pressure, gestational diabetes, varicose veins, and back problems, among other conditions—besides adding to the usual fatigue and physical discomfort that are associated with pregnancy.

How much is enough—but not too much? As with weight standards in general, the pendulum has swung back and forth over the decades. Believe it or not, at one time, it was medical protocol to advise a pregnant woman not to gain more than 18

Your Body As Public Domain

Pregnant with her first child, Susan, 34, a San Francisco communications consultant, was standing in line to renew her driver's license at the department of motor vehicles when a woman in an adjacent line cast an appraising eye on her midsection. "Is your baby due any day now?" the woman asked. When Susan told her the baby wasn't due for another two-and-a-half months, the woman replied: "Wow!—you're huge. How much weight have you gained?"

Having gained 23 pounds by then, her weight was well within the expected range, but that's not the point. Normally people wouldn't dare ask a woman how much weight she's gained; it would be considered bad manners. But during the long nine months of pregnancy, no subject is considered off-limits when it comes to the curiosity of strangers. People don't think twice about asking whether you've had morning sickness, whether you're still having sex, whether you're going to have natural childbirth, or even whether you plan to have another child after this one. Nor do some people have any hesitation about coming up and patting your belly. Why is that? For one thing, pregnancy is a very public event in the sense that it's so visible—and sometimes people want to share in the experience. Women often bond over the shared experience and bask in each other's excitement over the impending event. Others feel they have a vested interest in the next pounds. But doctors now recognize that this isn't enough for the baby's health and well-being. Currently the American College of Obstetricians and Gynecologists (ACOG) recommends that women gain the following amounts of weight during pregnancy: A woman whose weight is in the normal range should gain between 25 and 35 pounds; a woman who is underweight, by contrast, should gain 28 to 40 pounds, while a woman who is overweight should gain 15 to 25 pounds. (A woman who is carrying twins is expected to gain between 35 and 45 pounds.) Your

generation's well-being, one that supersedes a woman's right to privacy. So they remind her not to drink alcohol or smoke cigarettes—or do any number of things they believe, rightly or wrongly, might harm the baby.

Usually such invasions of privacy are simply an annoyance, but they can make a woman feel as though she's living under a microscope or that she's simply a vessel for the baby she's carrying. And this can feel stressful. Ideally, it's best to take the high road in such situations—and simply shrug them off with silence and a tolerant smile; after all, it's not worth wasting your energy responding to such intrusive types. But if you start to feel like a sitting duck and upsetting comments really start to get under your skin, it may help to seize a modicum of control by having a snappy retort at the ready. If someone remarks upon how much weight you've gained, you might say something like "It's so kind of you to notice; no one's told me that." Of course, if someone really crosses a line of permissible probing—by asking about your sex life, for example—there's nothing wrong with responding, "That's none of your business." All in all, though, it's a good idea to try as best you can to let such comments slide by without getting a rise out of you. After all, it's good practice for the round of nosy questions and unsolicited advice that's sure to come after the baby arrives.

best bet is to discuss how much weight you should try to gain with your doctor or midwife. Usually women gain about 7 to 10 pounds during the first 20 weeks of pregnancy and approximately a pound per week after that.

Of course, if you're overweight, pregnancy is not the time to try to shed pounds. It's essential to gain the right amount of weight for the sake of your baby's health and development. (For this reason, pregnant women are excluded from membership in Weight Watchers.) After all, the average healthy baby will weigh in between 6 and 8 pounds at birth; plus, the mother will store about 7 pounds in fat, protein, and other nutrients; 4 pounds in extra body fluid; 4 pounds in increased blood volume; 2 pounds in breast growth; 2 pounds for the enlarged uterus; 2 pounds for the amniotic fluid surrounding the fetus; and about 1 1/2 pounds for the placenta, which nourishes and removes waste from the fetus. (Much of the extra body fat is likely to be carried around a woman's hips and thighs; that's because hormone levels basically act like traffic cops and direct fat to the best storage areas until it's needed for breastfeeding.) All of these gains are essential for a healthy pregnancy.

Working Out During Pregnancy

Not so long ago, pregnant women were advised to avoid exercising and to take it easy. The fear was that exercise might increase the risk of miscarriage or possibly cause harm to the baby. Now doctors know that it's perfectly safe for healthy expectant mothers to exercise—within limits. In fact, moderate exercise is actually beneficial for the mother. Pregnant women who are fit and strong often have fewer aches and pains, as well as greater energy and self-esteem. Feeling fit can also make you feel more prepared psychologically, emotionally, and physically for labor and delivery. Of course, staying fit during pregnancy won't guarantee an easy delivery. A marathon runner stands no better chance of having a natural (drug-free) delivery than a couch potato—or of delivering vaginally rather than needing a cesarean section. But feeling fit can provide an enormous boost to your state of mind and can-do spirit—no matter how arduous your labor might turn out to be—which is a great way to begin motherhood.

How to get started? Slowly and carefully. Even if you're in triathlon shape going into the pregnancy, the experience brings about significant physiological changes that can affect your ability to participate safely in certain types of physical activities. For example, during pregnancy, your body temperature is higher than normal; your pulse rate is faster than usual; and your oxygen requirements are greater (because of the baby) than when you weren't pregnant. In addition, your center of gravity will shift, thanks to your growing uterus and breasts, which can affect your sense of balance. And your joints and ligaments will gradually loosen up, courtesy of surging hormone levels, which could increase your chances of injury. But these changes shouldn't discourage you from exercising; they should simply serve as a reminder to be careful.

Of course, you'll want to get your doctor's clearance before you start working out. If yours is a high-risk pregnancy—or if you have pregnancy-induced hypertension, a history of preterm labor, or an incompetent cervix—you may need to cut back on your activities or even stop exercising altogether for a while. Even if you're having a normal pregnancy and you're in good shape to begin with, your doctor may advise forgoing such risky activities as horseback riding or downhill skiing out of concern about your falling.

Assuming you do get the green light to exercise, certain forms of aerobic activity are considered ideal choices. These include walking, hiking, swimming, and cycling on a stationary bike. Gentle weight training is usually considered safe if you've been doing it since before you were pregnant but double-check with your doctor to be sure. As a rule, regular, moderate exercise—performed at least three days per week—is better and safer than the weekend-warrior style of activity. In addition, expectant mothers should frequently perform gentle stretching and toning exercises to relieve stiffness or muscle aches and to prepare for the big event. In particular, Kegel exercises, in which you squeeze, hold, then relax the muscle that controls the flow of urine, should be performed daily to strengthen the muscles in the vaginal and perineal area; this will help prepare you for childbirth, as well as decrease the risk of urinary incontinence.

Handling the Fourth Trimester

After giving birth, many women expect their bodies to snap right back to their prepregnancy shapes. And while a fortunate few can slip into their prepregnancy jeans by their six-week postpartum checkup, many new mothers need to wage a battle to get rid of the extra pounds and fat they've accumulated. Which is far from easy in the first few weeks and months of the postpartum period, often referred to as the fourth trimester.

For one thing, whereas a pregnant woman needs only 300 extra calories per day to nourish her baby, her daily caloric requirements actually increase if she's breastfeeding. A nursing mother will want to increase her calorie intake by about 500 calories above what she typically consumed before pregnancy. Those extra calories are required for the mother's bodily needs and personal energy level as well as to produce high-quality milk for the baby. So this isn't the time to go for quick weight loss. On the contrary, good nutrition is essential because in the beginning you're the baby's sole source of nourishment. (A nursing mother can become a member of Weight Watchers so long as she loses no more than an average of one pound per week after the first three weeks and follows an adapted 1•2•3 Success Plan that accounts for the increased nutritional needs of breastfeeding.) "While I was breastfeeding, I continued to eat healthy," says Ginny. "I started working out and tried to reassure myself that the weight would come off eventually, which it did."

If you've gone straight to bottle feeding, however, that's another story. It's perfectly safe to try to lose weight shortly after the baby's born, but stick with the slow but steady approach—meaning up to two pounds per week—rather than a quick fix with a fad diet. Quick weight-loss plans don't work over the long haul, and you certainly don't want to jeopardize your nutritional health while taking on the care of a newborn.

Even if you're nursing, that doesn't mean you can't begin to take steps toward reclaiming your prepregnancy shape—and the best way to do that is by exercising. The truth is, in the early weeks and months of parenthood, the idea of working out may seem about as appealing as having a root canal. After all, when you're trying to get through the day on two- to three-hour chunks of sleep and your body's still recovering from the rigors of childbirth, exercise is probably the least appealing pastime. But even doing something as gentle as a 15-minute walk can boost your energy and help your body begin to recover its prepregnancy form. Exercise can also help you cope with your mounting responsibilities and beat depression during the postpartum period. In fact, a recent study from the University of Michigan found that exercising after the birth of a child improves a mother's sense of well-being, both physically and emotionally.

The key is to start slowly; this isn't the time to push yourself physically. Many of the physiological changes, including loose joints and ligaments, that you experienced during pregnancy will persist until four to six weeks postpartum. Walking regularly and doing gentle abdominal-strengthening exercises, as long as you have your doctor's okay, are probably your best bets until your six-week postpartum checkup. At that point, if your doctor gives you the official go-ahead, you can probably begin to resume more vigorous activities, such as jogging, weightlifting, swimming, playing tennis, and so on. One of the biggest challenges is going to be finding time to fit exercise in once you have a young child, but it's doable if you use some creativity to find what works for you.

Gwen, for example, began rising at 5:30 A.M. five days a week to ride the stationary bicycle or use the treadmill in her basement for 45 minutes before her kids woke up. Within nine months, she'd not only shed the 53 pounds she wanted to lose but became an exercise convert, too. Try easing exercise into your baby's schedule with activities such as running with a specially designed baby carriage, doing an exercise tape while the baby naps, or joining a gym with babysitting services.

Getting Through Pregnancy
Without Sabotaging Your Figure

Now that you're aware of the pregnancy-related factors that can lead to unwanted weight gain, you can devise strategies to avoid these minefields. This doesn't have to be complicated. It's simply a matter of thinking ahead about the choices you make when it comes to diet and exercise, rather than just coasting through the nine months. Here's how:

1. **Stick with a healthy diet.**

Since you're nourishing your child as well as yourself, it's extra important to make healthy food selections. An easy way to do this, according to ACOG, is to continue to follow the U.S. Department of Agriculture's Food Guide Pyramid but to aim for the higher end of the spectrum when it comes to servings. For example, the pyramid recommends that a nonpregnant person have between 6 and 11 servings of bread, cereal, rice, and pasta per day; during pregnancy, try aiming for at least 9 servings. Next, have at least 4 servings from the vegetable group and 3 from the fruit group (you can't go wrong with more, though). At the third tier, consume at least 3 servings from the milk, yogurt, and cheese group (you need calcium now more than ever!) and at least 3 servings from the meat, poultry, fish, dried beans, eggs, and nuts group. At the top of the food pyramid are fats, oils, and sweets, which you should continue to consume sparingly; even now, you should get no more than 30 percent of your daily calories from fat.

What does a serving consist of? One serving from the bread, cereal, rice, and pasta group equals 1 slice of bread, $^1/_2$ cup of cooked cereal or 1 ounce of ready-to-eat cereal, or $^1/_2$ cup of cooked rice or pasta. One vegetable serving consists of 1 cup of raw leafy vegetables or $^1/_2$ cup of cooked or chopped raw veggies, while a serving of fruit is equal to 1 medium apple, banana, orange, or peach. One cup of milk or yogurt or 1$^1/_2$ ounces of natural cheese counts as a serving from the dairy group, and 2 to 3 ounces of lean meat, fish, or poultry or 1 egg equals a serving from the other group.

If you find full meals hard to stomach, it's fine to eat mini-meals throughout the day, so long as your total intake adds up to the recommended number of servings from these basic food groups. To ensure that you eat a variety of foods and get all the vitamins, minerals, proteins, carbohydrates, and fats you need, it might help to sketch out a daily food plan each morning. As insurance, your doctor will probably recommend that you take a daily prenatal vitamin. Finally, don't forget to drink plenty of water, at least eight cups per day. Your body needs more fluids than usual while you're pregnant.

2. Stay fit.

As you undoubtedly realize, pregnancy, labor, and delivery are arduous events that will be easier if you're physically fit. So if you've been exercising, keep it up in moderation; if you're new to exercise, start slowly—by walking or swimming laps at a comfortable pace, for example—and gradually build up from there. If you like to take exercise classes, choose those that are specifically designed for pregnant women, since these account for the physical changes and limitations imposed by pregnancy. In recent years, many health clubs, community centers, and hospitals have begun offering prenatal exercise classes for aerobic workouts, yoga, even water aerobics. You can also consider (with your doctor's okay) trying a prenatal exercise video. In any case, check with your obstetrician before exercising during pregnancy.

When you get the go-ahead, aim for consistency. Exercising four times per week is much healthier and safer than working out erratically. Even short bouts of exercise—walking on errands instead of driving, for example—can increase your fitness quotient and help you prevent excessive weight gain.

Because of the physiological changes that take place during pregnancy, a few precautions are in order:

• DON'T EXERCISE ON AN EMPTY STOMACH. If you like to head out for an early morning walk, have something to drink and a light snack 15 minutes or so before you go. Otherwise, you may feel light-headed while you're out.

- **WEAR SUITABLE ATTIRE.** Choose loose clothing in fabrics that allow your body to breathe and sweat to evaporate. And always wear appropriate footwear—walking shoes for walking, aerobic shoes for an aerobics class, and so on—to protect your joints and feet.

- **DON'T OVEREXERT YOURSELF.** Even if you're in great shape, pregnancy isn't the time to exercise to your full capacity. Try the talk test periodically while working out: If you can't carry on a conversation comfortably, you're pushing yourself too hard. So know when to ease up—and when to call it quits. If you feel lightheaded, dizzy, nauseated, out of breath, fatigued, or if you feel pain anywhere, stop immediately. (If the feeling doesn't go away after a brief rest, call your doctor.)

- **CHILL OUT IN HOT WEATHER.** When the mercury or humidity soars, skip an outdoor workout. Otherwise, you risk becoming overheated, which is dangerous for you and the baby. Head to the gym or the pool, instead—or try a pregnancy exercise video in your air-conditioned home.

- **DRINK UP.** Be sure to consume plenty of water before, during, and after exercising. For every 30 minutes of activity, you'll need at least a cup of fluids to replace what you've lost through perspiration or breathing.

3. Monitor your weight gain.

If you consume a healthy diet and exercise regularly, you'll decrease your odds of gaining too much weight. But keep an eye on the scale, nonetheless. The idea isn't to obsess about every pound you put on but to be aware of gaining trends. Weighing in once a week is plenty; step on the scale more frequently, and you may get a skewed picture of what's going on, especially if you're retaining water after a salty meal. If you gain a little more than you'd hoped in a particular week, don't freak out; just try to get back on track the following week. If you have trouble with overeating or managing your rate of gain, talk to your doctor.

4. Pamper your body.

If you find yourself struggling with body-image issues, it helps to pick a part of your body you're pleased with and play it up as much as possible. Say your legs continue to be shapely during pregnancy. You might treat yourself to a maternity mini-dress or two so you can show them off. Or if your long, slender neck is your strong point, buy yourself a pretty scarf or a choker to flatter it. The idea is to find what measures make you feel most attractive and put them into practice as often as possible. After all, you deserve to feel your best throughout these nine months.

5. Bolster your body image.

Look at your whole body each day and try to get used to the changes. Research has found that people generally accept the parts of their body that they look at most frequently. Applying lotion regularly can also help you grow more comfortable with your changing shape as you nurture it with hands-on care. Also, remind yourself that this is one time when you should have complete faith in your body. It knows what to do naturally, without your controlling it; that's something to be proud of.

Of course, it's also important to realize that it's not just your body but your whole life that's changing. The best thing you can do is surrender to these changes and allow yourself to visualize how you want to be as a mother and what you consider an attractive mother to look like. As your role changes, your standards of beauty should, too.

6. Keep exercising after the baby comes.

If you're planning to breastfeed your baby, the postpartum period isn't the ideal time to go for a quick weight loss. Your calorie requirements actually increase—by 500 per day—to produce good-quality milk for the baby and to meet your body's needs. But regular exercise can begin to coax your body back to a nonpregnant shape as well as help you cope emotionally with all the new demands and stresses placed on you. Start with a simple routine such as walking and gradually step up the pace and the length of your strolls as you feel ready. Hold off on resuming vigorous activities like jogging, swimming, or lifting weights until your doctor gives you the okay at your six-week postpartum checkup. Even then, don't expect the pounds to drop off immediately. Cultivate patience with the weight-loss process by allowing yourself at least the same amount of time to lose the weight as it took to put it on—that is, another nine months.

Do You Eat Out Your Stress on the Job?

Over the last five years, Susan, 26, a laboratory technician at a world-famous medical institution in the Midwest, has gained 70 pounds. The main reason, she says: work-related stress. "My job is very stressful," she explains. "In the beginning, I would eat

because I was afraid of making mistakes; it had to do with fear and feeling insecure. As time went on, the stress shifted. In my job, I train new doctors and researchers who come to work at the lab, and we always have deadlines for research and grants. We're always under the gun because if we don't get the information, we don't get the money we need to do our research. Plus, I have a hard time saying no, which means I tend to spread myself too thin with commitments or with handling problems that come up."

The trouble is, "I eat when I'm stressed," she continues, "and I've done it my whole life. It just got worse with the stress of this job. So it's been easy to gain weight. If I'm having a bad day at work, I'll hit the fast-food joints and the bakeries during my lunch break. I'll take a break and go out for a snack because we're not allowed to eat in the lab. Then I continue the pattern at home. I eat whatever I want—usually things like macaroni and cheese or enchiladas—in larger portions—sometimes twice as much as normal—because I think I deserve it. Eating gives me something to think about besides what pains in the neck the people at work are. But it doesn't usually make me feel better. While I'm doing it, I know I shouldn't be, and afterwards I'll feel bad because I know I shouldn't have done it. But it's not an easy habit to give up."

No matter what line of work you're in, you undoubtedly encounter stress on the job. In fact, a national survey by a life insurance company found that 25 percent of employees view their jobs as the number-one source of stress in their lives. Moreover, 75 percent of employees believe that today's workers have more on-the-job stress than the previous generation did, according to a survey by Princeton Survey Research Associates. Whether it stems from long hours, deadline pressure, too much responsibility, hotheaded bosses, colleagues who don't do their fair share of the work, pay inequities, competing for promotions, or hitting the glass ceiling—these days the world of work is rife with stress.

And some of the sources are unique to women. After all, women are more likely to be the victims of gender discrimination or sexual harassment in the workplace. And women have certain work-related frustrations to contend with that men simply don't. Even in 1999, for example, women still earn only 75 cents for every dollar a man earns, and 61 percent of women report that they have little or no opportunity for job advancement, according to the U.S. Department of Labor. Moreover, a 1997 study from Canada concluded that achieving a higher socioeconomic status "through work is a much more stressful process for women than for men and that women's upward mobility is restricted compared to that of men."

For both sexes, however, work-related stress can take a toll on physical and emotional well-being. Indeed, research has found that job strain can have a powerful effect on all sorts of health behaviors. For example, in a 1997 study involving more than 3,800 men and women from 32 different workplaces, researchers from the University of Minnesota found that highly demanding jobs were associated with increased smoking and fat intake among men and with increased smoking and higher body mass index (BMI) among women. And the more pressure the women felt on the job, the higher their BMIs tended to be.

Meanwhile, other studies have found an association between job stress and additional risk factors for cardiovascular disease. Research has found, for example, that working women who experience high levels of stress on the job are at increased risk of developing stroke, high blood pressure, and problem-drinking habits. And in a 1996 study, researchers from Yale University examined the relationship between employment status and cholesterol in 541 women ages 42 to 50. Both employed and unemployed women had similar cholesterol and health behaviors at the beginning of the study, but over the course of three years, those who were employed experienced a significant drop in HDL cholesterol, the good kind that carries harmful LDL cholesterol out

Working at Home

Warning: Whether you're self-employed or you're telecommuting, working at home can be hazardous to your weight. Why? First of all, you have unlimited access to food. The refrigerator is just a room or two away, and it's there all day long, which can make around-the-clock snacking—whether it's out of stress, boredom, anxiety, or frustration—or even cooking—whipping up a batch of brownies, for example—highly tempting. After all, you don't have the social support of an office environment to ease these feelings. "I'm a pro at eating whatever I can get my hands on quickly," says Grace, 37, a San Francisco writer who works at home. "When I don't have time to eat lunch or I'm stressed out, I'll eat whatever is the most emotionally satisfying thing that's lying around— potato chips, nuts, or cookies. And I'll just keep eating handful after handful until I'm full."

Plus, women who work at home often do so in their jeans, sweats, or other comfortable clothing. Which means they don't have the appearance-driven incentive to stay slim. Instead, their attire may put them in a lounging mood psychologically, which also can trigger the munching habit.

Another potential pitfall: Working at home often means there's little structure to your workday. After all, you don't have regular staff meetings to attend, an appointed lunch hour, or other time-slotted activities during the day. That's why it's important to get yourself into the right frame of mind before sitting down at your desk. How? By scheduling your day in a daily planner, just as you probably would if you worked in a company office, and by giving yourself a lunch break—whether it's used to meet a friend, to run errands, or to sit down to a solo meal at the kitchen or dining room table (not at your desk). It also helps if you plan your lunches ahead of time—or better yet, prepare them the night before, just as you would if you were brown-bagging it to the office. That'll take the spur-of-the-moment guesswork out of what's for lunch.

of the bloodstream. What accounted for the difference? The researchers concluded that employed women experienced this HDL decline primarily because they were less likely to increase exercise and more likely to gain weight than those who weren't employed.

The Definition of Job Stress

The question of what makes a job stressful may seem to be a subjective one. But researchers have developed a definition: "Job stress is defined as the harmful physical and emotional responses that occur when the requirements of a job do not match the capabilities, resources, or needs of the worker," according to the National Institute for Occupational Safety and Health (NIOSH). One measure of job strain, called the Karasek model, is based on the balance between the psychological demands a job places on a person—referred to as *job demands*—and the authority or ability a person has to address those demands—referred to as *latitude*. Job demands reflects the amount of work that's placed on a person and whether she's subjected to conflicting demands, insufficient time to do her work, or a hectic work pace, among other factors; latitude encompasses task variety, the ability to learn new things and develop new skills on the job, the level of creativity involved, and the freedom to make decisions, among other components.

According to this model, there are four types of jobs. When job demands and latitude are both high, an employee's skills and sense of control are adequate for the job, in which case workers tend to be stimulated and motivated to develop new, presumably healthy behaviors both on and off the job. People whose jobs place low demands upon them but also give them low latitude tend to be in passive positions; these workers often experience a gradual decline in activity and general problem-solving skills. Those whose jobs aren't very demanding but offer plenty of latitude for control and decision making usually experience low levels of stress and strain at work. In contrast, people who work in highly demanding jobs with little latitude—meaning their ability to use their skills or authority to address those demands is insufficient—are the most stressed out of all; not surprisingly, these types of jobs tend to have the most negative effects on a person's health.

In a 1997 study, researchers from the Duke University Medical Center in Durham, North Carolina, found that female employees of a local corporation who experienced high levels of demands on the job but didn't have much latitude in making decisions experienced increased levels of negative emotions, such

Workplace Wellness Programs

In recent years, many large companies have introduced workplace wellness programs—ranging from stress-management training and employee-assistance programs to cancer screening and fitness activities to nutritional counseling and even weight-loss programs (such as Weight Watchers). Participation rates are often low, however, even with the well-designed programs. A 1996 study of work-site wellness programs at a large petrochemical research and development company found that most programs attracted 10 to 40 percent of the company's employees; interestingly, women participated at higher rates than men did in all programs. Meanwhile, a 1996 survey of more than 3,000 employees in 10 federal agencies found that 17 percent of employees participated in agency-supported fitness-related activities and 40 percent in health-risk assessment activities.

Why the relatively low attendance? Perhaps it's because employees don't feel they have the time for such activities, or perhaps they're simply not aware of them. But they may be short-changing themselves. Although research has found that these programs may not significantly improve a person's satisfaction with her job, they can have a considerable impact in boosting her health.

as anxiety, anger, depression, and hostility. In addition, these women generally experienced reduced levels of social support and had more negative than positive feelings regarding their dealings with coworkers and supervisors.

"I've almost totally bagged exercise for the last year, mostly because my work is so demanding," says Nancy, 35, a financial analyst in Washington, D.C., who gained nearly 20 pounds during that time. "I changed bosses a few months ago, and I work long hours during the week and often on the weekends. Colleagues frequently ask me to help on projects and it's not an environment

For example, a work-site intervention program that was designed to increase fruit and vegetable consumption was quite effective, even more so when family members were involved, according to a 1999 report. Specifically, the group that was assigned to the work-site intervention program—and also received a written learn-at-home program and periodic mailings—had increased their fruit and vegetable intake by an average of 19 percent two years later. Meanwhile, in a 1999 study involving 1,162 people, researchers from the University of Massachusetts Medical School gave participants either normal medical care; nutrition counseling from their physicians; or physician-delivered nutrition counseling coupled with an office-support program. After a year, those who received physician-delivered nutrition counseling *plus* office support showed the greatest improvements in the percentage of their diets that were derived from saturated fat and in their blood levels of LDL ("the bad") cholesterol. In addition, this group experienced an average weight loss of five pounds; the other groups didn't. Clearly, some of these programs can help people clean up their eating habits and improve their health.

where you can say, 'No, I'm too busy.' You have to be a team player. I often have to travel for my job, but I don't always know when I'll be going because my travel schedule hinges on other people's; so it's hard for me to plan ahead. All this stress really makes me tired, so I started using my time off to rest instead of exercise."

Among the factors that can modify these stress levels—for better or worse—is the amount of social support a person receives at work, from both coworkers and supervisors. In a 1998 study, researchers involved with the ongoing Nurses' Health Study at Harvard University found that women who experience high levels of job strain along with low levels of social support tended to have the poorest health status, especially in the areas of fatigue, energy, and mental health.

Of course, different women react differently to work-related stress but there do appear to be some patterns in the way of dietary changes, in particular. Women who are naturally thin and don't worry about their weight often don't change their eating habits or eat slightly less when they're under stress, according to researchers. Women who do watch their weight, on the other hand, tend to respond by eating more. No one knows exactly why this is so, but one theory maintains that since chronic dieters typically try to limit their food intake, this self-controlled behavior becomes harder to maintain in the face of stress. In other words, stress releases the self-imposed brakes these women have placed on their eating habits. In addition, research suggests that ego-related stresses—such as having a performance appraisal or giving a presentation at a meeting where people will be evaluating you—are more powerful triggers for stress-related eating than are inconvenience-related stresses, such as getting locked out of your office. Which isn't surprising considering that more is personally at stake—namely, your reputation—with ego-related stresses.

Aside from stress, the way in which people generally work these days can also affect their weight. A century ago the average caloric intake was higher than it is today, and yet the obesity rate was substantially lower. The reason: People burned off those extra calories in the course of making a living. After all, working hard used to mean a person would expend more energy—and hence burn more calories—back in the days when we were an industrial or agricultural society and work required more physical activity and labor. Now working hard typically means putting in long hours sitting behind a desk, which doesn't expend much in the way of calories. And with the dawning of the computer age, workers have become even more sedentary. It's no longer necessary to walk across the office to deliver a memo, for example; instead, you can simply send and receive e-mail messages.

What's more, as people spend more and more time at the office or take work home with them in the evenings—a common response to the ever-increasing expectations companies have of employee productivity—many people find themselves scrambling to pull together meals. As a result, you may find yourself ordering pizza or Chinese food for delivery, microwaving frozen entrees, or eating fast food on the run more frequently than you'd intended. And chances are, you may not be putting a lot of thought into these choices; you simply go for what's easy, what's convenient, or what appeals to your taste buds at the moment— factors that don't always promote weight control. In fact, in a 1998 study of nearly 3,000 adults, researchers from the University of Hawaii and the University of Denver found that people frequently choose to eat the foods they do based first on taste, followed (in order) by cost, nutrition, convenience, and then weight control.

Worse, many diligent workers skip meals to finish a report, squeeze in extra phone calls, or catch up on reading while everyone else is out of the office; then, when they succumb to intense hunger, they might raid the office vending machine or their own personal snack drawer, which may not contain the healthiest choices. Or they may find themselves absolutely famished at the next meal and overeat at that point. And with coffee breaks often the only time for authorized social interaction, some people snack during these breaks in an effort to prolong them.

"I used to work at a magazine that had a casual social hour starting at 4:30 on Fridays," says Carolyn, 35, an editor on the West Coast. "It was a really stressful place to work, largely because the top editor was extremely difficult to work with, and this social time was considered the only legitimate reason to quit working that early and slack off. So we'd all go to the conference room, where there was a whole spread—platters of cheese, meats, and crackers; veggies and dip; bowls of cookies and candy; and lots of drinks. And because people were so relieved that the week was almost over, we would gorge, almost mindlessly. Then at 5:30 on the dot everyone would hightail it out of there to start their weekends. It's no wonder I gained weight in the nine months I worked there."

The Threat of Getting Fired

Losing your job—whether it's due to your own poor performance or company-wide cutbacks—is perhaps the ultimate form of work-related stress. Not only is it a threat to your livelihood, but getting fired is also stressful because it can take a toll on your self-esteem and sense of self. After all, we live in an age and a culture in which who you are is defined, to a large extent, by what you do. When that's taken away, even temporarily, it can lead to an identity crisis. In fact, a 1987 study of shipyard workers from Sweden found that people who became unemployed often went through a series of psychological crises that stemmed from how work contributed to their sense of identity—in their eyes and in the eyes of other people; not surprisingly, many of the laid-off workers became depressed. Similarly, in a study of blue-collar women who lost their jobs, researchers from the University of Pittsburgh School of Medicine found that those who were laid off also tended to be depressed during the 12-month study period; what's more, women who received poor levels of support from their significant others right after the layoff and those who experienced greater financial difficulties as a result of the layoff tended to experience deeper levels of depression.

Besides the effects on mood, when you lose a job, you often lose the sense of structure that's been imposed upon your life for however long you've been in the workforce. Suddenly there are hours and hours of free time to fill—and some people, apparently, use that time to eat and eat and eat. A 1992 study from the Royal Free Hospital School of Medicine in London found that people who became unemployed were significantly more likely to gain more than 10 percent of their body weight over five years than were those who remained employed.

But you don't need to be handed a pink slip to be at risk for gaining weight as a result of job insecurity. Even the possibility of losing a job can lead many people to begin packing on extra pounds. In a 1998 study involving more than 10,000 white-collar workers ages 35 to 55, researchers from the University College London Medical School discovered that having an uncertain future in the workplace can cause women and men to gain weight. At the time of the study, the government had called for an examination of civil service functions to see which could be abolished altogether and which could be transferred to the private sector; for those that were transferred to the private sector, the company was permitted to give a month's notice to any employee whose skills were no longer required. Among both men and women working under these conditions, there was a significant increase in body mass index (BMI) but an even greater one for women. On average, women facing job insecurity saw their BMI increase by over one point during the period of uncertainty.

In these days of corporate takeovers and mergers, uncertainty is often a fact of the modern working life. You may feel relatively secure today, but you may not know if your job—or even if your company—will still exist next month or next year. Working under the constant threat of losing your job—especially if coworkers are

Employees Who Rise Above the Fray

In studies of business executives, researchers have found that people who possess a quality called *hardiness* are less prone to depression, anxiety, burnout, and illnesses. What's more, a 1988 study of employees from two companies found that hardy individuals had higher levels of job satisfaction and fewer tensions at work than their less hardy counterparts; plus, the hardy souls reported a higher quality of life and a more positive disposition in general.

What makes people hardy? Generally, they have a commitment to being deeply involved in their life's activities and believe that these pursuits are interesting, important, and meaningful, which provides a general sense of purpose that can buffer them from stress, according to Salvatore Maddi, Ph.D., a professor of psychology at the University of California at Irvine. They share the conviction that with some effort they can influence a situation's outcome for the better. And they embrace challenges as opportunities for personal growth and gain, rather than viewing them as threats. As a result, they perceive changes in the workplace as much less stressful—and so do their bodies.

There's good news. Even if you've been pulled down by the undertow of workplace stress in the past, you can learn to bounce back better and faster in the future by cultivating the following qualities and skills:

• **Insight:** If you get in the habit of asking probing questions, you'll develop a keen sense of intuition and a deeper understanding of yourself and others. This will help you figure out what you can change and what you can't, and it will help you learn from past ordeals—all of which can help you anticipate and possibly sidestep work-related crises in the future.

• **Flexibility:** If one tactic doesn't work, don't be afraid to try another—even if it's risky or unusual—to get through a predicament. If you're preparing a report for tomorrow's staff meeting, for example, and your theme just isn't working, rather than panicking, you might consider scrapping the current approach and trying something more outlandish.

• **Humor and creativity:** By helping you turn reality inside out, humor and creativity allow you to regain perspective in the face of adversity—by realizing how cartoonish your boss is acting at the moment, for example—as well as helping you arrive at novel solutions to problems. What's more, psychologists have found that these imaginative qualities can also provide a safe mental haven in taxing times.

• **Empathy:** A sense of empathy helps you understand the dynamics of a relationship, learn from other people's experiences, and develop a good sense of timing. Indeed, the ability to read and understand what is going on with other people has helped many successful employees avoid becoming casualties of corporate takeovers, gauge when it's a good time to ask for a raise, or put their best foot forward for promotions.

• **Morality:** Maintaining an internal moral compass can help you navigate through sticky situations—like vying with a colleague you're friendly with for a certain promotion. Not only does it help you act with decency and compassion, but a sense of personal morality is a powerful source of energy and direction through hard—and easier—times.

• **Proactivity:** If you can't change a particular problem, find another one to work on instead. Taking action can improve the quality of your life, of course, and it can bolster your sense of control and your sagging spirits during a crisis. Best of all, it puts you in the driver's seat of your own brilliant career—and your life—which is as it should be.

losing theirs—can take a toll on your physical and emotional health, as well as your weight. That's why it's important to have a contingency plan in case you lose your job and to take steps to ease the stress you may be feeling under such conditions.

Dealing with Job Stress Without Stuffing Yourself

Whether your work involves short-term stress—your boss frequently loses her cool, for example—or ongoing stress—you usually have too much work to do in too little time—it is possible to get the job done without sabotaging your weight. What you'll need to do is find ways, even small ones, to sneak in exercise and to plan ahead when it comes to meals and snacks. And when stress strikes? Instead of giving in to the siren call of the vending machine, you need to have better ways to cope at your disposal. Here's how:

1. Give yourself a time-out.

When your stress meter registers "Overload" but you just can't do anything to get rid of the source, the urge to nosh for comfort can be practically irrepressible. And, if given a choice of what to eat, you'll probably gravitate toward sweets, carbohydrates, or high-fat foods. But indulging will probably make you feel worse in the long run. A better approach: Give yourself a breather before reaching for that candy bar. Look at what happened and see if you can gain a better perspective on the situation or find a way to learn from it. If a silver lining just isn't there, put the scenario out of your mind for the moment and give yourself a ten-minute break. Most cravings last about ten minutes, so if you can impose another activity for that long, the craving is likely to pass. If it doesn't, find a way to have just a small amount so you don't feel deprived but don't end up bingeing either. Keep items like Hershey's kisses around for such emergencies; eating a few won't harm your diet, since they have only 25 calories apiece.

2. Map out your meals.

Before stress gets to you, make sure you stick with a healthy high-carbohydrate, low-fat meal plan and eat three meals a day with two small snacks. If you need to be alert in the afternoon, have protein—in the form of a lean meat sandwich, for example—at lunch. It's also a good idea to include plenty of antioxidant-rich fruits and vegetables—aim for at least five a day—to protect your body from the harmful effects of stress. And watch your caffeine intake. In some people who are sensitive to it, caffeine actually mimics the stress response, causing more anxiety.

3. Exercise regularly.

You've heard it before but it bears repeating: Exercise can work wonders in relieving stress. Not only does it spark the release of pain-killing endorphins, but research also suggests that exercise can stimulate the release of serotonin and other mood-enhancing brain chemicals. What's more, exercise improves blood and oxygen flow throughout the body, which can also reduce stress. To keep yourself on an even emotional keel, try to exercise for at least 30 minutes most days of the week—either before or after work or during your lunch break. Recently Nancy, the Washington, D.C. financial analyst, began walking to work in the mornings, which takes her half an hour. "I enjoy it," she says, "because it relaxes me and puts me in a good frame of mind to start the day." Another option is to forgo your lunch break and head to the gym. You can also squeeze in short bouts of exercise—taking the stairs instead of the elevator at your office building, for example, or getting off the bus a few stops early and walking the rest of the way—for added fitness and stress-management benefits.

4. Stock your snack drawer with healthy choices.

Good items to keep on hand include packages of low-fat microwave popcorn, small servings of pretzels or dried fruit, individual boxes of dry cereal, or cups of soup. And for sweet-tooth emergencies, have a favorite fun-size candy bar, small bag of jelly beans, or package of sugar-free cocoa mix available. It's also a good idea to keep a bowl of fruit—oranges, pears, bananas—on your desk.

5. Develop your own stress busters.

When stress catches you by surprise, it helps to have relaxation strategies ready to help you calm down quickly. Otherwise, the body's fight-or-flight response will kick in. The hypothalamus in the brain will trigger the release of adrenaline, cortisol, and other stress hormones, which in turn causes your blood sugar, blood pressure, heart rate, and body temperature to rise. This puts your body into a super-alert mode, preparing you to fight or run for your life, which just isn't helpful when you're dealing with job stress.

That's why it's smart to nip this response in the bud—as soon as you feel your adrenaline begin to rush—by doing deep-breathing exercises, meditation, or progressive muscle-relaxation exercises (concentrating on systematically relaxing each major muscle group from your head to your feet). The key is to find what works for you—what helps you calm down and feel grounded—and to carve out at least 15 minutes a day for that activity.

6. Improve your coping skills.

When a crisis looms at work, your first instinct may be to try to solve the problem. But if you can't do anything to remedy the situation right away, your best course of action may be to not dwell on it. Research has found that rumination is more common among women, and it may partly explain why women are twice as prone to depression as men are. A wiser strategy may be to distract yourself from the problem—or at least your feelings for a while—by exercising, engaging in a hobby, or talking to a trusted friend, and to set worry hours for later, when you can go back and address the problem more constructively. At that point, write down what you're worrying about along with potential solutions to help structure your thoughts. If you can't do anything about the situation, try to come to terms with it the best you can or learn from the experience. This plan of action can help you cope better with difficult experiences.

7. Ask for help.

If work-related stress sends your eating habits out of control and you can't get them back on track yourself, it may be time to seek assistance. Since Nancy began working with a nutritionist last spring, she's been steadily losing weight. Meanwhile, Susan, the laboratory technician from the Midwest, has lost 40 pounds through Weight Watchers. Or you might benefit from professional counseling. Getting help with handling your eating habits or emotions won't automatically put an end to stress-related eating, but it can make it easier for you to apply the brakes on such behavior.

Changing Scenery, Changing Weight?

It was after her husband's third job transfer that Deanna began having problems with gaining weight. Because her husband is in the Air Force, she knew that relocation would be a fact of married life, but with each move, it didn't get any easier. "Every time we move,

we're back to ground zero," says Deanna, 49, a library assistant in Norfolk, Virginia, and the mother of three children. "Starting over all the time is the hardest challenge. I have to start over with my friendships. There's the stress of selling a house, buying a new home, packing up and moving, and worrying about my kids' happiness. And every time we move, I'm starting over with a job. Any pattern or routine we had is gone, which makes it hard to eat healthfully."

Not surprisingly, Deanna's weight has traveled up and down the scale—fluctuating by as much as 70 pounds on her 5'4" frame—as she and her family have crisscrossed the country and even the globe, thanks to a stint in Korea. Typically, the family moves every four years; Deanna has now lived in eight different locations during the 28 years of her marriage. "I usually gain weight when we move, and my weight has gone up with each move because I haven't lost the weight from the previous move," she confesses. "There's typically a lot of fast food involved as we're packing up, in transit, and getting settled. Everything I know I should do goes out the window. And the same is true with exercise. I used to play tennis religiously or walk with a friend, but every time I move, I lose all the people I play tennis or go walking with. So moving disrupts my exercise routine, too."

There's just no getting around it: Moving ranks pretty high on the scale of life's stressful events—literally. A few decades ago, psychologists developed what's called "The Social Readjustment Rating Scale," which assigns a value to various traumatic life events—such as the death of a spouse, divorce, a major personal injury or illness, a major change in living conditions, and being fired from a job, among others—based on how life-altering they are. While a change in residence isn't nearly as stressful as the death of a spouse—by itself, moving is about one-fifth as stressful, according to the scale—the amount of stress can quickly add up if the move also involves a major work adjustment, a major change in recreation or church activities, or significant changes in the frequency of family get-togethers. And depending on how you *feel* about relocating, that can either increase or decrease how difficult the adjustment will be.

In a 1999 study, researchers from the Karolinska Institute in Stockholm, Sweden, tracked the adjustments among a group of employees who relocated from Sweden to a foreign country because of a work-related assignment. Not only did the people who relocated experience a decline in mental well-being, but they also experienced physical repercussions, including increased levels of circulating stress-related hormones, such as prolactin and testosterone. Not surprisingly, the biggest changes occurred during the first year. And those who had a tougher time lacked social support and inner resources from which they could draw strength.

Pulling the Rug Out from Under You

It's really not surprising that moving can wreak such havoc on a woman's sense of well-being. After all, whether you move locally or relocate to another part of the country (or world), life goes through a period without structure. Gone are the familiar routines, the comforts of your previous home, the social connections you had with your immediate neighbors and community. Eating patterns often become erratic while you're living out of boxes. You may not know where to shop for food, and even the availability of some of your favorite foods may be quite different if you've moved from one region of the country to another (or to another country altogether). Similarly, your exercise habits can fall by the wayside. You may not know where it's safe or physically comfortable to go jogging or walking. And since moving to a new home doesn't usually bring with it an instant health-club membership, you may not have a clue about where to work out. And let's face it, joining a gym isn't usually your first priority when you're trying to get settled in a new home.

Even when the move doesn't involve traveling thousands of miles, the seemingly simple transaction of buying a new home can be incredibly stressful. And this, too, can affect a woman's eating habits. "Between the time we made the offer and we closed the deal on our house in 1995, all I wanted to eat was macaroni and cheese," says Georgia, 29, an environmental consultant in northwestern New Jersey. "It was a really difficult period for about four months. All the financial stuff was stressful, but the uncertainty—about whether we'd get the house and the mortgage—was the worst part. My husband was also stressed out. He was on the phone for at least an hour a day with the lawyer, the mortgage company, the insurance company, and so on. He just tried to keep me informed about what was going on, but I think I caught his stress, too, because I'm very empathetic.

"I internalized a lot of this stress because my family was so far away [in the Midwest]," she adds. "I didn't have anyone to vent to and food became my crutch. I started eating bigger portions and lots of bread with dinner—carbohydrates were like medicine; they were so soothing. I also started snacking more—eating tortilla chips, going to the candy machine at work in the afternoon. I probably gained 20 pounds during that four-month period."

Once the boxes are unpacked, the furniture is in place, and life begins to settle down, a woman's eating habits may not automatically return to normal. After all, emotional issues often come into play, especially if she has moved to unfamiliar surroundings or doesn't know anyone in her new location. Feelings of loneliness and social isolation can easily set in—and numerous studies suggest that these feelings can be harmful to your health, affecting everything from your risk of heart disease to your longevity. What's more, loneliness and social isolation are often major triggers for emotional overeating.

It's hardly surprising that people often use food to comfort themselves when you consider that loneliness reflects a feeling of internal emptiness; filling yourself up with food can create the illusion of filling the void within. In a sense, food can become a lonely person's best friend, her trusted companion. But eating out of loneliness can lead to a downward spiral when you've moved to a new area. It can quickly cause weight gain, which can make you feel less comfortable with your appearance and less confident about going out to meet new people, and this, in turn, can increase your sense of isolation and loneliness.

Indeed, surveys have found that boredom and loneliness are the most common triggers for emotional eating among both normal-weight and overweight people. In addition, when research scientist Judith Wurtman, Ph.D., and her colleagues at the Massachusetts Institute of Technology conducted a survey of people regarding stress-related overeating, they found that anger, exhaustion, depression, and boredom were especially big triggers for women; frustration, tension, and worry were too, but to a slightly lesser extent. All of these emotions are incredibly common when you relocate to a new area.

"Loneliness is a big issue," Deanna confirms. "When you move to a new place, you don't have anyone you can call locally when you need someone to talk to. You have acquaintances, but you don't share your innermost feelings with them. It takes time to make real friends. So you tend to hold back your emotions and put on a front for your children." But these emotions often have a way of affecting a person's food choices—as Deanna well knows. "When I'm stressed out, I grab the quickest thing I can put my hands on," she says. "I generally open a bag of something—usually chips or cookies—that needs no preparation."

The trouble is, many people reach for handful after handful of their favorite foods when those stress-related cravings kick in. Research has found that women typically go for carbohydrates (like bagels and crackers) and sweets (like cookies, cake, and chocolate), which can lead to weight gain. And loneliness-related eating can be especially risky for women who are accustomed to watching their weight. In a study published in 1999, researchers at Lakehead University in Thunder Bay, Canada, conducted an experiment in which they induced specific

Quiz

Are You Lonely or Simply Alone in Your New Surroundings?

There's a big difference between being alone in a situation and feeling lonely. Being alone is a relative state of solitariness, whether it's by choice or due to circumstances such as moving; loneliness, on the other hand, generally involves feelings of depression, emptiness, or isolation because of a lack of meaningful companionship or social connection to others. Loneliness, in particular, can lead to emotional overeating as people try to fill the emotional void inside them with food. To figure out whether you feel lonely, read each statement and decide whether it generally applies to you by marking it True or False.

1. At work, at home, or at play, I usually feel somewhat in tune with the people around me.

2. When I'm upset, I often feel like there's no one I can turn to or talk to.

3. I often feel utterly alone in this world.

4. Generally, I feel like I'm friendly to people I work with and meet socially.

5. Even when I'm with a group of people, I often feel left out.

6. For the most part, I feel like I have at least a few meaningful relationships with other people.

7. At this point in my life, I don't feel close to anyone, which makes me sad.

8. I feel like some of my friends and family members really understand me.

9. I often feel like nobody really knows me.

10. In social situations, I can usually find some common ground—whether it's interests or ideas—with other people.

   Now tally up your responses, then read the corresponding analysis:

1.	T: 2	F: 1		6.	T: 2	F: 1
2.	T: 1	F: 2		7.	T: 1	F: 2
3.	T: 1	F: 2		8.	T: 2	F: 1
4.	T: 2	F: 1		9.	T: 1	F: 2
5.	T: 1	F: 2		10.	T: 2	F: 1

17 to 20: Building Meaningful Ties

You seem to feel in sync with at least some people in your life—whether they're in your new or old location or somewhere else altogether. This means you have a portable support system—after all, there's always the phone—one that will help you weather life's changes. It also looks like you have the social gracefulness and conversation skills that will help you make new friends and acquaintances wherever you go. Don't be afraid to use your support system—or to rely on yourself. You won't regret it.

13 to 16: Holding Uneven Connections

It looks like the quality of your relationships tends to vary considerably. Some appear to be meaningful and gratifying, while others seem to be superficial, at best. If the balance feels too off-kilter, you may feel lonely sometimes. Maybe you should try opening up a little more easily and letting other people get to know the real you. Or maybe you should focus on drawing others out—an easier strategy for shy people, in particular—so that you can discover what you have in common. You might be surprised by what you find.

10 to 12: Keeping Others at Arm's Length

It appears there's a shortage of close relationships in your life, and that's not good for your health or your waistline. Maybe you don't open up to other people because you feel that you can't trust them, or maybe you lack the confidence it takes to be friendly and outgoing in new situations. Instead of making snap judgments about others or assuming they'll reject you, give them a chance. To boost your self-esteem in new situations, talk up your strengths and unique qualities to yourself beforehand, almost as if you were recommending yourself for a job.

moods—loneliness, sadness, or neutral feelings—in the female participants, then offered them cookies under the pretext that they'd be participating in a taste test. What they found is that women who typically exercise dietary restraint—they feel they need to consciously restrict their food intake in order to prevent weight gain—consumed more cookies when they felt lonely than when they felt sad or neutral. By contrast, those who weren't accustomed to dieting did the opposite—they ate fewer cookies when they felt lonely.

Easing the Wear and Tear on Your Body

Between bending over and packing up your prized possessions, lifting and hoisting boxes, and pushing furniture around, moving involves a considerable amount of strain on your body. And you may be using muscles, even entire muscle groups, you're not accustomed to placing demands upon. At the very least, this can lead to delayed onset muscle soreness (DOMS), which typically occurs 24 to 48 hours after a workout. It's the result of temporary damage to muscle fiber cells, which, in turn, produces an inflammatory reaction that causes pain.

DOMS is entirely normal and may be unavoidable to a certain extent, especially with movements that involve lengthening of the muscles (lowering a box to the floor, for instance, or walking down stairs carrying a box in front of you). But it could set you up for weight-related trouble. At the end of a day, you may find yourself eating to try to refuel or ease the severe soreness you're feeling when what your body really needs is rest. Another risk: If you do subject your body to excessive strain during a move, you may injure yourself, putting yourself on the disabled list as far as exercising in the following days (or weeks) is concerned. Indeed, if you're not careful, straining those unconditioned muscles could lead to acute injuries, especially to the lower back.

Moving to an entirely new area can also place a strain on a marriage, especially if you hardly know a soul in your new surroundings. You and your spouse may become more dependent on each other for a while and may feel the extra burden if you don't have other outlets—people to turn to, places to exercise in, enjoyable things to distract yourselves—from your stress. "It's very hard on a marriage," Deanna agrees. "Aside from the usual adjustments, your spouse has the stress of a new job, and he may tend to throw himself into that"—which can leave you to fend for

What can you do? First of all, to prevent serious injury, be sure to protect your lower back by bending from the knees (not the waist) and keeping your back upright and your head erect as you squat, lift, and carry. Whenever possible, use mechanical aids—such as carts or dollies—to move heavy objects or get assistance from another person to move heavy boxes. And if you feel any undue pain, stop what you're doing.

To minimize DOMS, try to rehearse the movements you'll be making a day or two before the crucial days, using light resistance. If you ease into the process by spending a day or two packing and carrying lighter boxes, that should help. Then work up to the heavy loads. It also helps to warm up—by doing a light aerobic activity such as walking or riding a stationary bicycle—for five to ten minutes, then stretch your muscles at the start of the day, as well as after a day of moving. Concentrate on stretching the muscles in the lower back, shoulders, hamstrings, calves, and quadriceps.

If you wind up with muscle soreness despite your best efforts, place ice on the sore areas and rest afterward. Having a massage also may help. If you're really uncomfortable, talk to your doctor about taking an anti-inflammatory drug, such as ibuprofen. Rest assured, the soreness won't last forever; DOMS usually goes away within three days.

yourself emotionally. Even the possibility or uncertainty of relocating can tax your relationship, especially if the marriage is on shaky ground to begin with. On the other hand, drawing on your personal resources and family support and appreciating your spouse's ability to cope seems to buffer some of the stress felt by couples, according to a 1999 study of couples living under the threat of forced relocation in Israel.

The Power of Place

The risks of gaining weight don't always end once you grow accustomed to your new surroundings, though. Depending on where in the country you wind up moving, your chances of adding pounds may be even greater than in your previous location. After all, research has found that excess weight and sedentary habits are more common in certain geographic areas than in others. The states with the highest percentages of adults who were obese in 1996 include Alabama, Iowa, Kentucky, Louisiana, Michigan, Mississippi, Missouri, Ohio, and South Carolina, whereas Arizona, Colorado, Kansas, Nevada, Utah, and Washington were among the states with the lowest obesity rates, according to the Centers for Disease Control and Prevention.

Some of these differences may be due to regional foods and cultural traditions, but the population's exercise habits may also play a role. In Washington, D.C., for example, more women are completely sedentary—that is, get no formal exercise—than in any other location, according to a report from the Jacobs' Institute of Women's Health; by contrast, Colorado boasts the highest percentage of women who exercise. Meanwhile, Hawaii has the lowest percentage of overweight women and Indiana has the highest. So if you adopt the lifestyle or mindset that's common to your new environment, you could find your weight changing along with your habits. In other words, the place where you live can have a powerful impact on your weight and health practices.

Making the Move
While Watching Your Weight

While you're moving and trying to get settled in your new surroundings, your life may not feel like your own. But you can get through this period of upheaval without letting it take an excessive toll on your eating and exercise habits. Your best bet is to seize a modicum of control by brainstorming about how you can maintain at least some of the healthy habits you've developed—by thinking ahead about the choices you make for your meals, finding small ways to fit exercise in, and seeking other sources of relief (that don't involve the kitchen) for stress, loneliness, and frustration. Here's how:

1. Hire as many helping hands as you can afford.

To ease the stress of moving, it's a good idea to have as many people help as possible—maybe someone to assist with the packing and unpacking, a house-cleaner for both locations, and perhaps a babysitter (if you have young children). That way, you won't feel pressure to be in ten places, doing ten different tasks, at once.

2. Create a routine.

Even though relocating can throw a once predictable life into a state of chaos, you can impose some sense of order—by keeping diet-related essentials handy (in a marked box that you can easily lay your hands on when you get to your destination) and by eating regular meals and snacks. Doing so will create a semblance of normalcy as you get settled in your new surroundings. It also helps to keep healthy snacks accessible—fresh fruit, dried fruit, microwave popcorn, small bags of pretzels, individual boxes of dried cereal, or containers of low-fat ready-made pudding. When you are forced to order fast food, take the healthy route: Skip the burger and fries and order a grilled chicken sandwich and a fruit salad instead; have a slice of pizza with veggies and forgo the meat toppings and extra cheese.

3. Shop wisely.

The stores may be unfamiliar but the aisles aren't—and neither are the packaged foods. So it's smart to use the same healthy shopping techniques you've heard about before—namely, shopping the perimeter of the grocery store, where the healthiest choices, such as produce, dairy, and the fish, poultry, and meat counters, are located. And, of course, continue to read labels on prepared foods—for both calorie and fat content.

4. Explore your new surroundings—on foot.

Maybe you haven't had time to find a gym you want to join, but that shouldn't stop you from exercising altogether. After all, you can probably walk right out your front door—and just keep going. Not only is it a great way to get to know your new neighborhood and do a little sightseeing, but walking can help you lose weight, too. Research from the American Cancer Society has found that a woman's body mass index decreases if she walks for a total of four or more hours per week. What's more, a 1997 study from the University of Florida in Gainesville found that women who walked at a moderate pace for 30 minutes, five days per week, from their homes, were more likely to stick with it after a year than those who joined a group walking program; not only that, but the home-based participants experienced greater weight losses after 15 months.

5. Make a distinction between being alone and being lonely.

You may not know many people where you've moved, so in that sense you may be alone. But that doesn't necessarily translate into loneliness, when you consider all the ties you have to various people, regardless of where they live. So stay in touch with people who matter to you, whether it's by phone or letter, and use this adjustment period to forge an even stronger bond with the person you're naturally closest to—yourself. As the French existentialist philosopher Jean-Paul Sartre once wrote: "If you are lonely while you are alone, you are in bad company." On the other hand, solitary time can be very gratifying if you use it to engage in activities that are meaningful to you—activities such as cultivating a new garden, writing in a journal, or sketching in the park. So make the most of the time you have to yourself—before you get completely absorbed in your new life.

6. Cultivate a can-do spirit.

And remind yourself of how strong you are. There's no denying that moving—whether it's to a new home, a new city, a new state, or a new country—is a big adjustment, but it can be made easier if your self-esteem is intact and you retain a sense of control over your life. In fact, the study of employees who relocated from Sweden to a foreign country found that people who maintain an internal locus of control—this means they feel like *they* make things happen, rather than feeling like things happen *to* them—and a strong sense of self-esteem had a milder physiological response to the stress of relocating, and they were better able to adjust to their foreign assignments. So when you feel overwhelmed, take a deep breath and talk yourself through difficult situations by using positive affirmations—such as "I can handle this" or "I'm going to make a good life for myself here"—that you repeat to yourself again and again, as needed. Giving yourself these personal pep talks will help you deal with the changes that are coming your way.

7. Get involved in the community.

If you went to church every Sunday where you used to live, find the nearest place of worship for your denomination and become a member. If you enjoy playing tennis or bridge, find a club or recreation center near you and sign up. If you enjoy volunteering, look for opportunities through a local church or volunteer agency. "You need something to look forward to, other than unpacking the boxes," says veteran mover Deanna, who recently lost more than 30 pounds—before moving again. "You have to be the one to go seek and find people. In today's world, people aren't going to knock on your door and say 'We're so glad you're here.' They're just too busy and wrapped up in their own lives."

8. Find healthy ways to release frustration.

When you crave comfort or need to de-stress, heading to the fridge or pantry is only likely to backfire, making you feel worse in the long run. Try a long soak in a bubble bath instead. Or go for a walk in a nearby park. Or put on some soothing music; call a friend from your old neighborhood; play with your pet; or buy yourself some flowers and arrange them in a pretty vase. There are many different ways to soothe yourself—ways that don't involve food—as you adjust to your new surroundings. It's up to you to discover what does the trick for you.

Will Quitting Cigarettes Send Your Diet Up in Smoke?

As an adult, Debbie had always been 25 to 30 pounds over her ideal weight, but her battle with the bulge really escalated when she tried to stop smoking. Actually, she had tried to quit at least five times, and with each attempt, she gained 10 to 15 pounds. Finally,

in 1994, she quit for good—and put on 30 more pounds in the process; by then she faced 90 pounds more than she wanted to see every time she looked in a mirror. "I think I gained weight while trying to quit because I was trying to satisfy the oral cravings with something else," explains Debbie, 45, a realty specialist in New Orleans. "But nothing else would do it because the craving was from nicotine addiction. I'd end up eating more to try to satisfy that urge—I'd try something sweet, then something salty, then something fatty—but nothing else worked."

Plus, "I wasn't as hungry when I smoked—it kept my appetite at bay," she adds. "A cup of coffee and a cigarette usually satisfied my hunger urge between meals and sometimes in place of a meal. Once I stopped smoking, I was ravenous. I started eating more at meals and for snacks. Part of it was also a matter of trying to find something else to do with my hands. When I was at a party, instead of lighting up a cigarette to go with my drink, I'd reach for hors d'oeuvres. In other situations, a few cigarettes would help me calm down. While I was trying to quit, I substituted eating. Food can be like a drug, too. I started eating a lot of chocolate—chocolate candy, chocolate cake, chocolate ice cream. I tried not to, but I felt like I was already depriving myself of one bad habit, so I figured I'd lose the weight when I got over this."

Without a doubt, smoking is one of the toughest habits to kick. Not only is it physiologically addictive—nicotine clearly meets the criteria of an addictive drug—but it can be psychologically, too. After all, nicotine has the unusual power to calm people down when they're upset or pep them up when they're tired. Indeed, smoking is a way of managing stress for many women. It can provide them with an automatic break, even a change of scenery, during a hectic day at work, especially if their office has a no-smoking policy and they have to go outside to light up. And it often sets up a smoke screen with family members at home;

giving in to the urge for a cigarette sends a loud and clear message that you need a time-out or at least a few moments to yourself. No wonder data from national surveys on drug abuse indicate that 75 percent of women who smoke feel they need or are dependent on cigarettes. Given these factors, it's also not surprising that 80 percent of those who tried to cut down on their cigarette consumption felt unable to succeed.

Compounding the addictive aspects is the fact that, as unhealthy as it is, many women use smoking as a tool to control their weight, which is why many are loath to give up the habit. A 1999 study involving 281 sedentary women who were enrolled in a smoking cessation program at Miriam Hospital in Providence, Rhode Island, found that the women relied on smoking as a way of controlling their weight primarily because the habit helped them eat less or because they were either worried about gaining weight if they quit or had put on pounds with previous attempts to quit. And their concerns are not unfounded.

After all, there is a physiological reason smoking can help a person prevent weight gain. Nicotine is a stimulant, and it does increase a person's metabolic rate, causing the heart to beat faster and the body to burn more calories, at least in the short term. Indeed, a 1995 study from the University of Memphis found that resting energy expenditure—the amount of calories a woman's body burns when she's just sitting around, performing basic functions like breathing—increased immediately after smoking a cigarette. In the first ten minutes, there was nearly a 10 percent rise in metabolic rate among smokers who were of normal weight and a 4 percent increase in metabolic rate among obese smokers. For a moderate smoker, this metabolic boost translates into burning about an extra 150 calories per day, according to researchers. At the same time that it revs up a person's metabolism, smoking also may blunt a person's appetite and dull her sense of taste, effectively removing some of the pleasure from eating.

Who Gains Weight after Quitting—and Why

There's no denying that many women do gain weight after they quit, although estimates on just how much of a gain is typical vary widely. Many women embark on smoking cessation efforts knowing this—and some are even willing to accept gaining a certain amount of weight as the price they pay for improving their health. For example, a 1996 study from the University of Michigan found that women were willing to gain about five pounds if they quit smoking. The trouble is, the reality often exceeds this—and sometimes considerably.

In 1998, for example, researchers from the University of Miami School of Medicine in Florida examined how much weight nearly 6,000 former smokers in the U.S. and Canada gained over five years. Among those who were able to quit without relapsing for five years, women gained a mean of 5.2 kg—nearly 11.5 pounds—the first year and a mean of 3.4 kg—equal to almost 7.5 pounds—after that; what's more, 19 percent of women who were sustained quitters gained 20 percent or more of their baseline body weight. In a 1995 study, researchers from the Centers for Disease Control and Prevention analyzed data on current and past weight and smoking status for 5,200 men and women around the country. What they found is that women who quit smoking gained an average of 5.0 kg (or 11 pounds) over a ten-year period. Meanwhile, a 1996 study from the Kaiser Permanente Medical Care Program of Northern California found that among 582 women participating in smoking cessation classes, the average woman gained 9.9 pounds over a one-year period while increasing her calorie intake for the first six months; interestingly enough, most women's calorie intake returned to normal by the one-year point.

But not all quitters are equally vulnerable to gaining weight after kicking the habit. It appears there may be something of a self-fulfilling prophecy at work here. In a 1998 study, researchers from Brown University School of Medicine in Rhode Island found that among people participating in a smoking-cessation clinic, those who were very concerned about gaining weight after kicking the habit were more likely to gain weight. Similarly, a 1998 study from the University of Toronto found that women who were veteran dieters gained considerably more weight after quitting than nondieters did. The theory? It may be that people who exercise high dietary restraint as dieters—they feel they need to consciously restrict their food intake in order to prevent weight gain—generally do increase their food intake and gain more weight after quitting smoking than those who don't. Meanwhile, a 1996 study from the Stanford University School of Medicine in California found that among people who had quit smoking, those who reported increasing symptoms of depression between quitting time and the two-year follow-up period experienced greater weight gain but were less likely to relapse.

Admittedly, part of this weight gain may be due to slight changes in metabolism. After all, once you give up cigarettes, you no longer get the short-term metabolic boost from nicotine. But much of this post-quitting weight gain has to do with how a woman's behavior changes after she stops lighting up. Research has found that people consistently consume 250 to 350 more calories per day after quitting. In addition, a 1996 study from the University of Minnesota found that smokers who quit increased their consumption of sweets, such as doughnuts, cookies, cake, and ice cream. "After I quit, I wanted to eat much more," says Willa, 59, a design consultant in Washington, D.C. "I became food-obsessed for a while because everything suddenly tasted better."

Looking for Incentive

While the number of adults who smoke in the United States declined between 1965 and 1990, it has remained virtually unchanged since then. In 1995, the number of cigarette smokers in the U.S. was 47.2 million, and almost 23 percent of American women smoked in that year, compared to 27 percent of men, according to the American Lung Association. Moreover, in 1996, nearly 14 percent of women who gave birth smoked during pregnancy, which is especially hazardous, considering that smoking during those nine months has been associated with low birth weight in babies.

Gaining a few pounds in the short run—as long as you can limit it to just a few—may be a small price to pay for reducing your risks of cancer of the lungs, mouth, esophagus, larynx, bladder, kidney, pancreas, and cervix, as well as heart disease, stroke, respiratory illnesses, premature wrinkling of the skin, and other ill health effects in the long term. Approximately 431,000 Americans die each year from diseases that are directly related to

The Psychology Behind Oral Gratification

This may ring a distant bell from Psychology 101: It used to be thought that smokers and overeaters were orally fixated. The idea was that these people developed an ongoing need to put something in their mouths because their oral needs were either undergratified or overgratified in early childhood.

But psychologists don't put much stock in this theory anymore, largely because there's no evidence to back it up. Besides, it's not clear why one person might use food to fulfill this oral need while another person might turn to cigarettes. Plus, when you consider the wide variety of oral behaviors people have—from chewing gum to drinking lots of lattes or bottled water to biting their fingernails—you'd be hard-pressed to find people who don't seem to have some need for oral gratification.

If you seem hooked on some of the less healthy oral behaviors, don't bother psychoanalyzing yourself. Simply try to replace them with less harmful options, such as drinking lots of water or low-calorie beverages, chewing sugarless gum, or sucking on sugarless candy. These won't harm your lungs or your waistline.

smoking, according to the American Lung Association. What's more, recent long-term studies suggest that about 50 percent of all regular cigarette smokers die of diseases that are related to the habit. If all this isn't enough incentive to quit, consider the dangers of secondhand smoke—to your spouse and your children, in particular. Secondhand smoke can cause health problems ranging from respiratory and middle-ear infections to bronchitis and pneumonia in youngsters. Plus, research has found that children whose mothers smoke a pack a day or more have twice the rate of extreme behavior problems as those whose mothers don't smoke.

The good news is, many health benefits begin to accrue shortly after you kick the habit. Your heart disease risk, for example, drops dramatically within three to five years of quitting smoking. Within two years of giving up cigarettes, the mortality rate for former smokers drops by 17 percent compared with those who continue to smoke, according to a report from the ongoing Nurses' Health Study at Harvard University. Research has also found that smoking cessation can improve a woman's cholesterol levels and dramatically improve lung function for both women and men. Moreover, in a recent study from The Miriam Hospital and Brown University School of Medicine, researchers evaluated the effects of smoking cessation on exercise performance in middle-aged women. What they found is that those who quit were able to exercise longer after 12 weeks than those who underwent the same exercise training but kept smoking. Not only that, but the women who quit also experienced a greater increase in their peak oxygen consumption, a measure of lung function. Clearly, the payoffs begin to kick in relatively quickly.

How Quitters Can Win

At any given time, 70 percent of smokers say they want to stop smoking, according to the American Lung Association, and 34 percent try to quit each year. The vast majority of those who try to kick the habit do it cold turkey—without professional help.

But after a year—which is considered the measure of success— only about 8 percent of them will have stayed smoke-free. In a 1997 study from the University of Memphis, researchers found that 62 percent of people who tried to quit smoking on their own returned to the habit after just 15 days; among those who made it through the 15-day period, women were more than three times as likely as men to relapse after that. Just why women might be more likely to fall off the smoke-free wagon is a mystery.

Why do so many attempts to kick the habit go up in smoke? For one thing, many people have unrealistic ideas about what quitting actually entails. It's not as easy as flicking a switch and being done with cigarettes once and for all. Kicking the habit takes time, patience, and perseverance, and aspiring quitters may need to try several times before they succeed. In fact, it takes most people four to six attempts to stub out the habit for good. The first three to six months are the hardest, according to smoking-cessation experts, partly because aspiring quitters haven't yet figured out other ways of comforting themselves besides lighting up. So if you can make it through this difficult window, you have a better chance of not going back to cigarettes. In fact, 85 percent of those who make it through a year without smoking don't return to the habit.

For people who don't want to quit cold turkey, plenty of help is available. Group programs may be able to maximize motivation for those who need ongoing support to quit—or for those who've tried unsuccessfully to quit on their own. Each program works a little differently, but generally they help smokers understand why they want to quit, explore various methods of quitting, and teach coping and stress-management techniques, such as relaxation and visualization strategies. Some programs even use high-tech support—in the form of phone calls or computer messages—to help smokers kick the habit. Over the long haul, program success rates vary; most are between 20 and 40 percent (a one-year success rate of 25 percent is considered good, anything above that is considered excellent).

Among the toughest hurdles for aspiring quitters to clear are nasty withdrawal symptoms, such as lightheadedness, sleep disturbances, constipation, headaches, anxiety, general irritability—and increased appetite. These alone sometimes send a person back to the habit. "When I tried to quit smoking, I felt like I had PMS all the time," Debbie recalls. "I was crying and I had serious mood swings. I was driving the people around me crazy." While it's long been believed that withdrawal symptoms gradually subside with time, new research from the University of Wisconsin-Madison Center for Tobacco Research and Intervention suggests that nicotine withdrawal symptoms can behave like monsters in a bad horror movie. Just when you breathe a sigh of relief, thinking you've destroyed them, they return with a vengeance. Indeed, it seems that withdrawal symptoms can resurface months after a person tries to quit smoking.

Fortunately, in recent years, smokeless nicotine—also known as nicotine-replacement therapy—has become available to help smokers gently wean themselves from the physiological addiction of nicotine. In addition, antidepressants such as Zyban have been found to be highly effective in helping people cope with the negative moods that often stem from withdrawal, thus making quitting a little easier. Indeed, by some estimates, treatments such as nicotine-replacement therapy and Zyban can double or triple a person's chances of kicking the habit for good.

How does nicotine-replacement therapy work? Attached with adhesive to the upper arm—almost like an oversized bandage—the nicotine patch releases nicotine into the bloodstream through the skin; some patches feature dosages that are gradually decreased over a period of time so that smokers can ease into breaking the physiological addiction. Chewing nicotine gum can also buy smokers time to work on breaking their psychological addiction without suffering withdrawal symptoms. To use it correctly, a person needs to steer clear of coffee, juice, and other acidic beverages for 15 minutes before chewing the gum, since

The Stages of Change

The secret to success when it comes to kicking a bad habit: using the right tools at the right times. For many years, psychologists James O. Prochaska, Carlo C. DiClemente, and John C. Norcross have studied how people make lasting changes in their lives—on their own, without the benefit of therapy. In their research, they have found that lifestyle changes appear to occur in six predictable stages—precontemplation, contemplation, preparation, action, maintenance, and termination—and that people who try to accomplish changes they're just not ready for typically set themselves up to fail.

If you can pinpoint your current stage of change, they've also found that you can then gain insight into the types of strategies that can help push you to the next stage—and help you maintain motivation.

Precontemplation: During this stage, you're probably resistant to change. You often deny there's a problem or rationalize why you should leave your current habits alone.

What to do: Think about all the self-defeating excuses that block your ability to make healthy changes in your life, and try to become aware of when you use them—and why. This is a good time to gather information about what constitutes a healthy diet and the benefits of giving up cigarettes, and to enlist the help of others.

Contemplation: At this point, you've probably become aware that a problem exists, and you've begun to think seriously about taking action. Yet on some level, you may still be resistant.

What to do: Consider why you want to change and what your real goals are. To build motivation, make two lists: one of the possible benefits of improving your habits (more energy, a healthier body) and another of the potentially harmful consequences of <u>not</u> changing your behavior (dying at a premature age, for example). Refer to this list to motivate yourself.

Preparation: By now your intentions to change are sincere and you're probably on the verge of taking action. You may even have taken small steps toward your goals—by cutting back on the number of cigarettes you smoke or how often you eat junk food. But you might be spending more energy on preparing mentally for what's ahead than on taking action.

What to do: Make changing your ways a priority in your life and tell your family and friends about what you plan to do so they're prepared to help. Then develop a plan of action that suits your lifestyle and incorporates helpful suggestions from others who've done it—and set a date to quit smoking or change your eating habits.

Action: This is when you swing into action and start modifying your habits and behavior. Even at this phase, change can be slow because it involves a major commitment of time and energy. So be prepared: Stumbling blocks will crop up.

What to do: Let your environment support you—by cleaning out your pantry and restocking it with nutritious foods or by trashing all your cigarettes. It also helps to introduce healthy substitutes—such as exercise or relaxation techniques.

Maintenance: The trick is to make the changes you've made permanent. To prevent relapses, focus on all the positive benefits you've reaped as a result of those changes—increased self-confidence, more energy, better breathing, and so on. When slip-ups happen, simply try to learn from them.

What to do: Prepare ahead for high-risk situations. If you relapse, initiate damage control immediately and renew your resolve.

Termination: By now you have complete confidence in your ability to handle difficult situations without lapsing into old patterns of eating or lighting up. Your new, improved habits have become an integral part of your life.

What to do: Lavish yourself with congratulations. Your hard work and persistence have paid off, and you're in a great position to handle whatever challenges come your way.

these can hinder nicotine absorption. It's also important to chew the gum slowly—for 20 to 30 minutes—for optimal benefits. Some people who use the gum, however, experience unpleasant side effects, such as throat irritation, gas, and hiccups. Both the nicotine patch and gum are now available without a prescription.

Meanwhile, two newer forms of nicotine-replacement therapy have become available by prescription only. One is nicotine nasal spray, which provides a quick hit of nicotine through the nasal passages; the downside is that some people experience nasal and throat irritation and sneezing with use of the nasal spray. The other new form is a nicotine inhaler that the aspiring quitter puffs on periodically throughout the course of a day; the advantage to the inhaler is that unpleasant side effects are much less common.

Success rates are basically comparable for the patch, the gum, the nasal spray, and the inhaler—generally in the vicinity of 15 to 30 percent. By themselves, however, none of these forms of nicotine replacement address psychological addiction, so it's a good idea to combine their use with visits to a support group or a doctor. Besides making quitting easier, there's more good news about these aids: Several studies have found that the amount of weight gained after quitting smoking tends to be lower among those using nicotine-replacement therapy.

In December 1998, Denise, 43, a nurse from the Chicago suburbs, used the nicotine patch for six weeks to help her quit smoking. Because she'd struggled with her weight for most of her adult life and carried an extra 30 pounds on her 5'1" frame, she was worried about gaining more after she quit; so she joined Weight Watchers the previous spring and lost 37 pounds by her quitting date. "Surpassing my weight-loss goal gave me confidence and motivation to quit smoking," she says. Though she gained about 7 pounds after quitting, she managed to stop the weight gain right there. How? "Using the patch helped ease my cravings, and I've exercised religiously during this whole period," she explains. "I do cardio work on the treadmill and work with free weights. That and drinking lots of water helped me the most. It made me feel healthier and sleep better. It was like a puzzle—everything just fit together."

Kicking the Habit
Without Adding Pounds

Have you used your fear of gaining weight as an excuse for not giving up cigarettes? Or have you quit smoking before but gone back to it *because* you gained weight? Although both of these are legitimate concerns, it is possible to quit this unhealthy habit and still stay slim. No, it's not easy. But it can be done. The key is to be on the lookout for troublesome situations you're likely to face—and to have a plan in place ahead of time for how you'll handle them. Here's how:

1.   Start a smoking diary.

Keep track of when and where you typically light up; this can give you insight into the emotional role the habit plays for you. The key, then, is to map out strategies to help you find either a way to distract yourself from the yen to smoke or an activity to replace the act of smoking. Once you know that you usually get the urge to puff when you're chatting on the phone, when you're having a drink at a bar, or when you're simply feeling

stressed out, you can try to engage in another activity until the craving passes, which usually occurs within ten minutes, according to experts. Chewing on a straw or a stick of gum, sucking on a cinnamon stick or a very strong mint, or keeping your hands occupied with knitting or needlepoint are a few of the tactics that would-be quitters use.

2.   Exercise regularly.

To begin with, working out can make you feel stronger and more up to the arduous task you're facing, which can make quitting easier. But starting to exercise regularly can also help you minimize weight gain while you quit smoking, according to a 1996 report from the ongoing Nurses' Health Study at Harvard University. In a study of nearly 1,500 women who stopped smoking, researchers found the average weight gain over two years was 2.4 kg, the equivalent of about 5 pounds; among those who quit and increased their level of physical activity so that they were exercising vigorously for one to two hours per week, the average weight gain was only 1.8 kg (about 4 pounds), while those who stepped up their physical activity so they were exercising vigorously for two or more hours per week tended to gain only 1.3 kg (a little less than 3 pounds).

The bottom line: Even moderate exercise can prevent the excess weight gain that's associated with quitting smoking. Moreover, in 1994 researchers from Memorial Hospital of Rhode Island compared the characteristics of smokers who attempt to quit and of those who succeed. They found that women were more likely to kick the habit successfully if they increased exercise and didn't live with a smoker.

3. Find other ways to deal with emotional upset.

Emotional distress is the most frequent reason people relapse and return to smoking, according to researchers. Which isn't surprising, considering that one of the most appealing aspects of smoking is that it provides instant gratification. When you're stressed out and temptation strikes, it may help to find a buddy to talk to, to practice deep breathing exercises, or to go for a brisk walk or a jog to sweat out a craving or relieve some of those unpleasant feelings. A 1998 study from St. George's Hospital Medical School in London found that using a buddy system with smokers who were trying to quit helped people abstain from cigarettes. Three weeks after their quit date, those who had a buddy were more than twice as likely to be free of cigarettes as those who attempted to do it alone. If you decide to use the buddy system, discuss with your partner how he or she can best help you at the outset.

4. Be patient with yourself.

When it comes to giving up a bad habit like smoking, you can't rush change—or else you're going to sabotage yourself. Research has found that people who fail often think they have something kicked within a short period of time when, in fact, it can take three to six months to get a new pattern established and even longer to solidify it. So take your time and don't beat yourself up about slip-ups— they're bound to happen. In a study of New Year's resolutions, researchers at the University of Scranton in Pennsylvania discovered that people who successfully changed their ways had the same number of slips as their unsuccessful counterparts during the first month, but the successful people forged ahead. In other words, they didn't let a lapse become a complete collapse. So if you're trying to quit smoking and one night you give in and have a cigarette, don't sweat it; simply put an end to it then and there and get back on track the next day.

5. Let your spouse know how to be helpful.

Just as social support can help people lose weight, the same is true of quitting smoking. But research has found that there's a right way and a wrong way to try to influence smoking cessation. In a 1996 study involving 624 people, researchers from the University of Minnesota examined how a spouse's supportive or undermining behaviors influenced his or her partner's efforts to quit smoking. They found that such behaviors as nagging or policing were likely to lead to a spouse's relapse, especially in the short term, whereas verbal reinforcements for the partner's attempt to quit or help with thinking of substitute activities for smoking were much more helpful. The key is to let your spouse know how best to help you at various stages of your efforts to quit.

6. Reward yourself.

The idea isn't to indulge in a hot fudge sundae for every week you've gone cigarette-free but to reward yourself in a way that doesn't involve food. Some aspiring quitters keep a special calendar posted and mark off each day they go without a smoke. Then at the end of a certain amount of time—a month, perhaps—you might buy yourself a small present—a new CD, a book, or an article of clothing—with the money you would have spent on cigarettes.

7. Tackle one challenge at a time.

In other words, don't try to do too much at once. Quitting cigarettes is hard enough without worrying about your weight. So smoking-cessation experts often recommend focusing your attention and energy on quitting first while making an effort to eat healthfully and exercise regularly. Then, once you've stayed cigarette-free for six months, you can deal with the scale and try to lose weight if need be.

That's what Debbie, the realty specialist from New Orleans, did. After quitting smoking permanently four years earlier, she joined Weight Watchers in 1998 and lost 107 pounds in less than a year. Not only did she change her eating habits, but she began exercising at least an hour a day. "While I was trying to quit, I figured gaining weight was the lesser of two evils," she explains. "Once I knew I'd quit for good, I decided to take the weight off. It was easier than if I'd tried to do both at the same time."

Minding the Menopausal Transformation

Though she'd struggled with emotional eating for much of her adult life, menopause turned out to be an enormous challenge for Judy. "When I first started taking hormones, my weight went up about five pounds, but I was also overeating," confesses Judy, 52, a

schoolteacher in northern California. "I was off the wall emotionally. I had terrible mood swings: I'd be high, I'd be low. I was depressed. And I'd eat nonstop—as soon as I got home from work, I would start in. I didn't want other people to see me eat; I would have been too embarrassed for them to see what I was eating. I was craving lots of high-fat stuff, things like bread with peanut butter, ice cream, and foods with butter or cream in them. I would eat enough in three hours to last for three days. And the more I ate, the more depressed I got. It got to the point where I didn't want to go out. I just didn't feel good about myself.

"Even when I watched what I was eating, I had a hard time losing weight," recalls Judy, who ended up gaining more than 30 pounds during menopause. "I had gained weight through the midsection, and the fat seemed to be showing more. I was exercising all that time, and when I used to exercise, I could lose weight, but this time nothing was working."

It's the final rite of passage in a woman's reproductive life—the onset of menstruation and pregnancy being the first two—but menopause isn't always greeted so warmly. Indeed, in The Healthy Women Study, which involves more than 500 premenopausal women, researchers from the University of Pittsburgh School of Medicine discovered that many women have downright negative expectations about some of the effects of menopause. Nearly 80 percent of the participants thought women are liable to become depressed during menopause; 68 percent thought women are more likely "to fly off the handle" during menopause; and about 75 percent thought that *all* women have hot flashes during menopause. Interestingly enough, the researchers found that there appears to be a self-fulfilling prophecy at work—that having negative expectations about menopause seems to affect the quality of the experience. That goes for the physiological and the emotional experiences—and it could have an effect on a woman's weight, too.

The Stages of Menopause

Many people think of menopause as a discrete event in a woman's life that's almost like crossing a threshold into another room. Suddenly there you are in the next part of life. But the truth is, menopause isn't nearly that abrupt. For most women, menopause is actually a transitional phase—more like a long tunnel than a doorway—that takes place in stages over a period of about ten years. In the perimenopausal years, which usually begin in the midforties, a woman's menstrual periods start to become irregular, often occurring more frequently than they used to. She may begin to experience hot flashes, insomnia, and mood swings, which can be alarming if she doesn't realize that the menopausal transition is underway. (There's some evidence that women who have suffered premenstrual syndrome may be more susceptible to mood swings during perimenopause.) Whatever symptoms a woman has, the perimenopausal stage generally lasts about four years.

After that, menopause, which is defined as the permanent cessation of menstruation, occurs. Since a woman's periods are likely to become very infrequent before they stop altogether, it's often difficult to gauge when menopause actually takes place. Once they stop completely—something that can often be realized only in retrospect—the ovaries have stopped producing estrogen. (Hormone levels can be tested to be sure a woman is truly menopausal.) This typically happens between the ages of 48 and 55, although the average age of menopause is 51. At this point, a woman's muscle mass begins to decrease and her percentage of body fat may increase, causing her metabolism to slow down. The result: weight gain.

A woman has officially entered the postmenopausal years when she no longer has menstrual periods. By this point, hot flashes are a thing of the past; gone, too, are the mood swings and other unpleasant symptoms that some women experience during perimenopause. In their place may be new symptoms such as dry skin and hair, vaginal dryness, and urinary incontinence. Of larger concern, however, is the rise in certain health risks—most notably a woman's risk of cardiovascular disease and osteoporosis—as a result of the loss of estrogen.

Granted, this timeline applies only to natural menopause. When a woman undergoes surgical menopause—after a hysterectomy and oophorectomy (removal of the uterus and ovaries)—the process is quite different. In this case, what she experiences is instant menopause, a sudden and dramatic drop in hormone levels, which may produce more severe symptoms across the board.

Weighty Matters

At this point, there's no definitive answer to the question of whether the hormonal changes that occur in menopause directly lead to weight gain. These are difficult studies to do—because of the lengthy time frame that's involved and the delicate issue of measuring hormone levels, among other factors—and the research to date has been relatively scarce. There is animal research, however, suggesting that estrogen does influence energy expenditure—specifically, that resting metabolic rate decreases as estrogen levels drop, as they do in menopause. At the same time, research with animals has found that voluntary physical activity generally decreases and calorie intake tends to increase as estrogen levels diminish. And estrogen is considered an appetite suppressant, so the drop in estrogen that comes with menopause may, indeed, stimulate appetite.

What is known more certainly is that menopause is considered a high-risk phase for weight gain in women. Research has found that the average woman gains two to five pounds during the entire menopausal transition, although some women see a much more considerable rise on the scale. Whether the loss of estrogen is actually to blame for the added pounds that often coincide with menopause is still under debate. But it is clear that many women find themselves battling a thickening of the midsection during this time of life, which, along with weight gain, can play an important role in a woman's subsequent health risks. Research has found that menopause leads to a redistribution of body fat; in particular, more fat is deposited in the abdominal region, which is more typical of men than women before menopause. (Premenopausal women, by contrast, tend to carry more fat in their hips, thighs, and arms than in the midsection, and that's because hormone levels are basically acting like traffic cops, directing fat to the best storage areas until it's needed for functions such as breastfeeding during the reproductive years.)

While a slight thickening of the waist is normal during menopause, carrying excessive fat in the midsection—the so-called apple-shaped pattern of obesity—is worrisome because it increases the risks of heart disease, hypertension, and diabetes, among other chronic diseases. But it's important to differentiate between this natural thickening of the abdominal region and actual weight gain. Just because your pants and skirts fit a little more snugly around the waist doesn't mean you've actually put on unwanted pounds. In fact, as the circumference of their waists becomes a little larger, many women assume they've gained more weight than they actually have. If your waistline has thickened but the scale hasn't budged, there's no need to worry.

The weight gain part of the equation is more complicated. In a 1991 study of nearly 500 women ages 42 to 50, researchers from the University of Pittsburgh tracked the women's weights over a three-year period. During this time, the participants gained an average of five pounds; 20 percent of the women gained ten or more pounds. Not surprisingly, this weight gain was associated with increases in blood pressure and blood levels of total cholesterol, LDL cholesterol, triglycerides, and fasting insulin—all of which increase a woman's risk of heart disease. Meanwhile, a 1994 study involving nearly 600 women from Italy found that body mass index (BMI) was significantly higher in peri-menopausal women than in premenopausal women; waist-to-hip ratio also increased among postmenopausal women.

Precisely what accounts for these changes isn't known. But it looks like a variety of factors may come into play. Indeed, there appears to be something of a domino effect on weight during these years. With increasing age, women, in particular, have a tendency to become more sedentary, and with a more sedentary lifestyle comes a loss of muscle mass and an increase in body fat. A 1992 study from the Wynn Institute for Metabolic Research in London found that postmenopausal women had 20 percent more body fat than premenopausal women did. Meanwhile, researchers at the University of Maryland and the Baltimore Veterans Affairs Medical Center found that body fat increases with age at an even greater rate for women than for men: at a rate of 5 percent per decade for women compared to 3 percent for men. This increasing accumulation of fat was most closely associated with decreased physical activity and physical deconditioning. And since muscle burns significantly more calories than body fat does—pound for pound, muscle burns between 35 and 50 calories per day at rest, whereas body fat burns only 2—a woman's resting metabolic rate decreases as she grows older and less active.

This is significant because resting metabolic rate regulates body weight, body composition, and a person's daily caloric needs; in other words, this age-related metabolic slowdown can have dramatic effects on a woman's body. In fact, a 1995 study by researchers at the University of Maryland and the Baltimore Veterans Affairs Medical Center found that lean muscle mass decreased by almost seven pounds and resting metabolic rate declined by approximately 100 calories per day in post-menopausal women. Unless a woman cuts back on her daily calorie intake or increases the amount of exercise she gets, this metabolic decline will undoubtedly lead to weight gain.

In addition, other factors may play a role in affecting how much weight a woman gains at this time of life. Research from the University of Pittsburgh has found, for example, that quitting smoking during the menopausal transition is associated with greater weight gain. What's more, a 1998 study from the University of Vienna in Austria found that women were more likely to be overweight—defined as having a body mass index over 25—during the postmenopausal period if they had experienced early menstruation and/or a late menopause, had children at an early age, and gained larger amounts of weight during pregnancies. (Interestingly, a study from the University of Massachusetts at Amherst found that women who had either lost 50 or more pounds or gained 100 or more pounds across adulthood typically experienced menopause at a slightly earlier age.)

The Silver Lining

If all of this sounds disheartening, don't despair. Here's a bit of good news: A woman can offset much of this age-related metabolic decline with regular exercise, both the aerobic variety and resistance training. In a 1997 study at the University of Colorado at Boulder, researchers found that endurance-trained swimmers and distance runners who were postmenopausal did not experience the age-related decline in resting metabolic rate that occurs in sedentary women, which explains why they weighed less and had lower levels of body fat than their sedentary counterparts. In addition, a 1995 study from the Jean Mayer USDA Human Nutrition Research Center on Aging at Tufts University found that performing strength-training exercises twice a week for a year led to substantial increases in muscle strength in postmenopausal women—and reduced the risk of osteoporotic fractures. Not only that, but over a year the participants gained three pounds of muscle. By lifting free weights, using machines such as Nautilus or Cybex, moving against gravity by doing sit-ups or push-ups, or performing exercises with rubber tubing or Dyna bands, a woman can add or preserve lean muscle mass at any stage of life, which will increase her resting metabolic rate and help her control her weight.

There is also some evidence that hormone replacement therapy (HRT) may prevent an increase in fat storage around the midsection after menopause begins. While some women believe that HRT causes weight gain, this may be mostly related to the water retention that's associated with the hormone progesterone. But there's no evidence that HRT actually causes a gain in body fat. Indeed, in 1998, two major studies—one from Australia, the other from Thailand—concluded that HRT doesn't cause weight gain; on the contrary, in the study from Thailand, participants who took HRT experienced a small reduction in body weight over one year. Meanwhile, a 1995 study from Israel found that HRT had absolutely no effect on body weight. It didn't prevent weight gain but it didn't encourage it, either; HRT did, however, minimize the redistribution of fat to the midsection. And a 1997 report from The Postmenopausal Estrogen/Progestin Interventions trial—also known as the PEPI study—found that among 875 women, those who took HRT gained an average of two pounds less after three years than women who took a placebo agent; women taking HRT also experienced slightly lower increases in waist and hip girth.

Besides these weight-related benefits, HRT protects against osteoporosis, heart disease, and Alzheimer's disease. In the short term, it can make your life a lot more pleasant as you go through menopause—namely, by reducing, if not eliminating, hot flashes and by improving vaginal dryness, which often occurs after the last menstrual period. Moreover, research has found that postmenopausal women who use hormone replacement therapy have a 30 to 50 percent lower risk of mortality from all causes than those who don't use HRT. It may, however, increase a woman's risk of uterine and breast cancer, which is why it's smart to discuss the pros and cons of HRT—and whether you're a good candidate for it—with your doctor.

The Emotional Adjustments

Independent of the mood swings that many women experience during perimenopause, some women become depressed. It's no secret that women are twice as likely as men to become depressed at some point in their lives, and the risk of depression does seem to be higher for women at times when hormone levels are changing. This may be because estrogen can influence the activity of serotonin and other brain chemicals in such a way that may have a mood-lifting or an antidepressant effect.

But hormonal fluctuations may not be entirely to blame for depression during the menopausal years. Depression in these years may have as much, if not more, to do with a woman's life circumstances. A 1997 study from the Center for Women's Health Research at the University of Washington in Seattle examined three factors that are linked to depressed mood—namely, the menopausal transition, stressful life events, and health status—among 337 women during midlife. It turns out that stressful life events played the most influential role in accounting for depressed mood among these women, and health status also affected depressed mood both directly and indirectly by increasing a woman's stress level. Menopausal changes, by contrast, were found to exert little influence on mood.

Yet, whether a woman undergoes menopause naturally or surgically, the transition can be an emotionally stressful period. After all, this marks the end of a woman's reproductive years, which she may feel sad about. Plus, given the average woman's life span of 75 to 80 years, menopause typically marks her entry into the final third of her life. And depending on what's currently happening in her life—her changing roles and responsibilities, whether her children have left home, or whether she's caring for aging parents—the milestone could make her begin to question herself or her goals for the future.

In 1994, Sherry, 46, a medical records custodian in Tucson, underwent surgical menopause through a hysterectomy and oophorectomy after being diagnosed with uterine cancer. Shortly after the operation, she began feeling blue, then her emotional well-being took a nosedive and she began to suffer a personal identity crisis, which affected her eating habits and her weight. "I had cravings that were similar to pregnancy," she recalls. "And I would snack all day long. First, I went on this incredible chocolate binge. Then I got disgusted with myself because I started gaining weight, so I stopped eating chocolate. Almost immediately the substitute craving was for butter. I would dip pretzels or crackers in a tub of soft margarine. I'd frost my toast or cover potatoes with butter. I could not get enough of it. I'd even bring a tub of soft margarine to work.

"I gained 35 pounds in four months—it was astounding," Sherry says. "Obviously, I was giving my weight gain all the fuel it needed. But it took me a while to realize that it was because I was depressed." Once she began feeling better emotionally— thanks to counseling and medication—she stopped bingeing and began losing weight.

Compounding the emotional ups and downs that many women experience at this time of life is a cultural reality. There's no denying that we live in a youth-oriented culture that prizes beauty, fitness, energy, and vitality. A culture where wrinkles are considered the enemy. Where women of all ages strive to have figures that look like they're eternally taut, toned, and only 20. Where the greatest compliment to a woman at midlife might be that she hasn't changed a bit since her college days. Where an older man is considered distinguished but an older woman is simply old.

It's as if looking one's age were the biggest curse in the world. And this can make it difficult for a woman at midlife to accept her changing face and body, particularly the plumping of the midsection she's fought against for so much of her adult life.

Indeed, many health experts now recognize that menopause is a vulnerable period for a woman's body image, just as adolescence, pregnancy, and the postpartum months are. Not only can it affect how she feels about her body, but her body image can color her entire life—her sense of emotional well-being, her self-image, even her health habits.

And a negative body image can stand in a woman's way of making healthy changes—ones that would benefit her health and weight. In a 1998 study, for example, researchers at Colorado State University found that postmenopausal women who experience high levels of social physique anxiety—meaning they become anxious when other people observe their bodies—were more likely to have a sedentary lifestyle, a high percentage of body fat, and more upper-body fat distribution, which often happens during menopause, than those who didn't feel socially anxious about their bodies. In other words, feeling anxious about their bodies may cause postmenopausal women to shirk physical activity. This can lead to a downward spiral. Being sedentary, particularly during the menopausal years, can increase a woman's percentage of body fat and lead to a decrease in muscle mass, which could cause her to feel worse about her body—which can make exercising in public even more difficult, and so on and so on . . .

On the other hand, having a healthy body image may protect against such unhealthy lifestyle habits. And at least a few studies have found that some women like or at least accept their bodies better as they age. Part of this effect has to do with a woman's sense of accomplishment in life. In a 1988 study, researchers at Virginia Polytechnic Institute and State University found that having a positive body image at midlife was associated with positive self-esteem—in other words, feeling worthy as a person—and a sense of life mastery—that is, feeling in control of your life.

Indeed, the stereotypical images of a menopausal woman being past her prime or mourning the loss of her youth don't have to become the reality. On the contrary, there are plenty of advantages to reaching this stage of life—having a new sense of freedom now that the children have left home, spending more

The Empty Nest Syndrome

Here today, gone tomorrow—that's what it feels like to many women once their children leave home and strike out on their own. It's not that child rearing flies by in a flash. It's more a reflection of the fact that women, in particular, often grow so accustomed to the commotion of having children at home that once they leave, the family home can seem oddly quiet, still, and empty. Moreover, a woman may feel as though her true life's work is done. In short, her life and environment can be dramatically transformed by the sudden departure of her children.

Sure, there are plenty of positive aspects to the change—more time with her spouse; the freedom to pursue new interests and goals; a cleaner, tidier home; more peace and quiet than she's had in decades. But the sudden reality that the children have left home, never to return permanently, can feel like quite a jolt. Not surprisingly, many women suffer emotional aftershocks, such as depression or loneliness, which can affect their physical well-being and eating habits. In her clinical practice, psychologist Joan Borysenko, Ph.D., cofounder of the Mind/Body Clinic at New England Deaconess Hospital in Boston and the author of *A Woman's Book of Life*, worked with hundreds of women who were negotiating such midlife changes. She found that those who were most prone to depression defined themselves primarily as mothers, gleaned most of their self-esteem from caring for their children, and weren't very involved in the world outside their children's activities. Moreover, these women often had poor relationships with their husbands, largely because they were so focused on their children. Not surprisingly, they felt emotionally adrift after their children left home.

Aside from these issues, it can also take women a while to adjust their routines to the new reality of having fewer bodies at time with your mate, and waving good-bye to fears about unwanted pregnancy, to name a few. This could turn out to be the

home. "My kids had gone off to college, one, two, three, and I continued cooking the same way," says Linda, 51, a teacher near Worcester, Massachusetts, who gained 10 pounds after her kids left home. "I'd cook enough for the five of us, and my husband and I would eat what was there so there were no leftovers. My husband isn't a dessert eater and I am, so when I'd make dessert, it would be just me to finish it off. Food is my security blanket when things aren't going well. I've always retreated to food choices like chocolate to comfort myself. All of my children went to school out of state, and I missed them. It was hard to let go; I wanted to but I couldn't."

Rather than trying to let go, it may be easier to pour more of your energy into new activities and passions once your kids leave home. Research from the University of Michigan has found, for example, that spending an hour or less per week helping others can prolong your life. The longevity benefits may come from the sense of meaning or purpose in life that people get from volunteering—or from the reduced risks of depression and loneliness that result from such activities. So this may be the perfect opportunity to begin volunteering at your church, at a local women's shelter, or another charity of your choice. In addition, this could be the chance you've been waiting for to challenge yourself to learn a new skill or language, to start exercising regularly, or to improve your eating habits, now that you have fewer people to care for directly. After all, isn't it time you started nurturing yourself as well as you have your children? That's what Linda finally did in 1997 before her daughter got married. After joining Weight Watchers, she lost 32 pounds—and now feels a lot more comfortable in her own skin.

happiest time of your life. A 1998 study from Fordham University in New York examined the midlife experiences of a group of women in the region along with what factors were associated with successfully negotiating the midlife transformation—and there were a few surprises. For one, 73 percent of the women described themselves as happy or very happy. What predicted these feelings of well-being? Having good health, a close confidante or a group of women friends, high self-esteem, goals for the future, a positive story to tell about one's life, inspiring midlife role models, and positive feelings about one's appearance all played a part.

The bottom line is, attitude seems to make a big difference in determining how a woman responds to menopause and the physical and emotional changes it engenders. Cultivating optimism may be a woman's best defense against depression, unpleasant physical symptoms, and weight gain. It's a psychological weapon that's worth arming yourself with, since women, in particular, are living longer, fuller, healthier lives than ever before.

Moving into the Last Third of Life Without Adding Pounds

While some women do struggle with their weight during the menopausal transition, weight gain doesn't have to be inevitable at this stage of life. As you now know, you can't blame your hormones entirely for whatever weight gain might occur during these years. At first blush, this may seem like bad news because it takes away a ready-made excuse. But it's actually good news because it means you can take steps to prevent much, if not all, of the weight gain you might otherwise experience. Here's how:

1. **Lose weight before you reach menopause.**

In an ongoing research project that was begun in 1992, researchers at the University of Pittsburgh have looked at whether initiating lifestyle changes in diet and physical activity can prevent the weight gain that often occurs during menopause. And so far it looks like the answer is yes. In the project, more than 500 women— some of whom are of normal weight, others of whom are overweight—were asked to lose at least five pounds by reducing their total and saturated fat intakes, lowering their calorie intake to between 1,300 and 1,500 per day, and exercising more so that they burned 1,000 to 1,500 calories per week through physical activity. All of the participants successfully lost weight, and researchers tracked whether they maintained their habits and slimmer physiques after 18 months. Although some of the weight had begun to creep back on, by 18 months 80 percent of those in the study still weighed less than they did when the study began. So it looks like making an effort to slim down before menopause actually takes place may pay off in helping you manage your weight in the post-menopausal years.

2. **Exercise regularly— aerobically, that is.**

Not only will it help you burn calories faster—both while you're working out and afterward—but it will help prevent the weight gain and physical deconditioning that often occur with advancing age. In fact, a 1996 study from the University of Manitoba in Canada found that when postmenopausal women walked briskly for 60 minutes three times per week, they experienced a 1 percent reduction in body fat after just 24 weeks. What's more, working out can help boost your mood as you navigate through this period of many changes. The key is to find activities you enjoy—then to stick with them. For Sherry, it was in-line skating; for you, it might be something else.

3. Begin a strength-training program.

If you aren't already lifting weights or performing other resistance training exercises, here's added incentive: Research has found that strength training adds and maintains lean muscle mass in postmenopausal women, which is one of the keys to metabolic efficiency as we get older. Research from the South Shore YMCA in Quincy, Massachusetts, has found that doing one set of 15 strength-training exercises just two times per week can lead to a gain of three to four pounds of muscle mass in two to three months for postmenopausal women. Gaining three to four pounds of muscle mass can increase a woman's resting metabolic rate by up to 180 calories per day—which can go a considerable way toward helping you control your weight. Judy now does resistance training three times per week and sees the difference. "I'm seeing more results," she says. "I look more toned and more muscular. Now I can see muscles beneath the skin."

4. Consider hormone replacement therapy.

Yes, it confers all sorts of health benefits, both in the short term—by relieving hot flashes and vaginal dryness, among other symptoms—and in the long term—by reducing your risks of heart disease, osteoporosis, and other chronic diseases. It also may prevent menopause-related weight gain, particularly the increase in body fat that typically occurs in the abdominal region. But hormone replacement therapy isn't for everyone. Your wisest course of action is to discuss the issue with your doctor to see if you're a good candidate and, if you are, to find out which of the many available protocols might be most suitable for you.

5. Look for positive role models.

These days, more and more women are aging not just gracefully but beautifully, successfully, and happily. Indeed, some women relish this stage of life; after all, they're relatively free of family responsibilities for the first time in decades. Moreover, many women experience what's come to be called "postmenopausal zest." The term was coined by anthropologist Margaret Mead, and it refers to a new surge of energy, vitality, power, and confidence that often follows menopause. To help yourself "catch" that empowered feeling, look for women around you who exemplify that sense of zest and try to learn from their attitudes and behavior. Then find ways in which you can pour that vitality and energy into aspects of your own life.

6. Appreciate your body.

Rather than focusing on any newly emerging imperfections you might perceive, focus on all that your body has done over the years—perhaps that it gave life to your children, that it lets you express affection physically, that it's probably allowed you to travel 75,000 miles on foot by the time you turn 50, among other accomplishments. Since many women have spent much of their adult lives trying to attain some impossible physical ideal of beauty, they're woefully out of touch with how beautiful they really are, at any age. So spend some time on a regular basis looking in a full-length mirror and taking note of your best features. At this point in your life, in particular, it's also important to focus more of your attention on your body's health. If you start leading a healthier lifestyle and nurturing your body properly—through healthy eating habits, regular exercise, and plenty of rest—you'll be treating your body with the love and respect it deserves. And you'll be putting yourself into the best shape possible as you enter the next phase of your life.

The Secrets of Staying Slim at Any Stage of Life

By now you know about the biological, psychological, and behavioral factors that can make you vulnerable to gaining weight during certain phases of your life. You know that the hormonal changes brought by pregnancy and menopause, for example, can lead to

permanent weight gain if you're not careful with your lifestyle habits. Similarly, an age-related decline in muscle mass—one that stems partly from becoming more sedentary with the passing decades—can also cause the number on the scale to creep steadily upward. And you've seen how emotional issues—involving struggles with stress, body image, loneliness, and depression—can also affect your eating and exercise habits for the worse. Now that you're blessed with all this awareness and knowledge, the question is, what are you going to do with it?

The fact of the matter is, if you want to lose weight at any stage of your life, you'll need to heed some basic guidelines. It's been a truism since the dawn of dieting—and it's never going to change: You need to expend more calories than you consume from food and beverages if you want to lose weight. If you take in more calories than you burn off, on the other hand, you'll gain weight. While it's true that genetics plays a role in determining a person's weight, there are still plenty of factors that affect your weight that are under your control—namely, your eating and exercise habits. Here's what you need to know about managing your weight under any circumstances, along with a two-week eating plan to help you do just that: expend more calories than you consume.

Nutrition 101: A Refresher Course

Proponents of many fad diets would like you to believe that some calories count less than others when it comes to weight management but there's no evidence that this is so. The truth is, every single calorie that enters your body can affect your weight; it's a nutritional fact of life, and it's completely democratic in the sense that it applies to everyone, rich or poor, heavy or slim. Whether you get them from carbohydrates, proteins, or fats, all calories count. The word "calorie" refers to the amount of energy a particular food gives your body. Ounce for ounce or gram for gram, different types of foods supply your body with different amounts of calories. A gram of protein and a gram of carbohydrates, for example, each contains four calories. A gram of fat, by contrast, has about nine calories, which explains why foods that are high in fat are also high in calories. And a gram of alcohol—which doesn't have any nutrients (that's why beer, wine, or spirits are often referred to as "empty calories")—has seven calories.

The Crux of Carbohydrates

Carbohydrates are your body's most potent source of energy, and they fuel your brain with energy in the form of glucose (or blood sugar). Which is one of the reasons why most of the country's top health associations now recommend that you get at least 55 percent of your daily calories from carbohydrates. But the quality of the carbohydrates counts as much as the quantity, since not all carbohydrates are created equal. There are the simple ones that are found in sugars, whether they're from fruits, certain vegetables, table sugar, or honey; these are easily digested by the body and provide a quick burst of energy that doesn't last long. Then there are the complex carbohydrates—found in rice, grains, beans, many vegetables, pastas, and breads—which take longer for the body to break down; as a result, complex carbs give you a more sustained flow of energy and help you feel full longer.

Another reason it's important to make good selections when it comes to carbohydrates has to do with dietary fiber. Carbohydrates in their "natural" state provide fiber. Processing tends to remove it, so a grapefruit and brown rice have lots of fiber; grapefruit juice and white rice do not. And fiber is important for your diet—both for weight loss and for your overall health—for several reasons. First, because it helps you feel full or sated. Second, because it helps keep things moving smoothly through your digestive tract, lowering your risks of constipation and other ailments in the process. In fact, research has found that a high-fiber diet can lower your blood cholesterol and decrease your risks of heart disease, high blood pressure, and Type II diabetes, among other health problems.

There are two types of dietary fiber. Soluble fiber, which is found in oats and oat bran, fruits, beans, barley, and other legumes, can help lower blood cholesterol, thereby protecting against heart disease. Insoluble fiber, on the other hand, which is found in whole-grain breads and cereals, wheat bran, and the skins of fruits and vegetables, passes through the digestive tract basically undigested while absorbing lots of water; as a result, eating plenty of insoluble fiber has a laxative effect and can reduce the risk of various digestive disorders.

Surveys have found that most Americans eat only half the daily fiber they should. The current recommendation calls for 20 to 35 grams of fiber a day, a combination of soluble and insoluble. That may sound like an impossible quota to fill, but it's easily achievable if you include at least one fiber-rich item in every meal: a bowl of high-fiber cereal for breakfast, a sandwich on whole-wheat bread with lots of veggies for lunch, a pear or a cup of strawberries for a snack, and a double serving of vegetables or one serving plus brown rice for dinner, for example. Be sure to increase your fiber intake gradually and drink plenty of fluids to help it move easily through your gastrointestinal tract.

The Protein Picture

Protein, which is composed of amino acids, is the body's major construction material. It's essential for building and maintaining muscles, blood cells, enzymes, hair, nails, and connective tissue, as well as disease-fighting antibodies in the immune system. It's also important for key body functions, like blood formation and the healing of wounds. The reason protein is so important is your body needs more than 20 different amino acids, 9 of which must come from your diet, the other 11 of which can be made in your body.

Yet, as important as protein is, most Americans consume more than they need, typically twice as much. The average healthy adult needs about .8 grams of protein for every kilogram (or 2.2 pounds) of body weight. That means a 140-pound woman needs about 51 grams of protein a day—an amount that is easily fulfilled by eating a lean broiled pork chop and a four-ounce serving of flounder on a given day. In recent years, protein has become unfairly equated with fat. While it's true that some protein sources—such as cold cuts and cheese—are high in fat, there are also plenty of low-fat options—such as fish, lean cuts of meat, yogurt, tofu, and black beans. So, as with carbohydrates, quality counts with protein, too.

Fat Fundamentals

These days, people seem to go out of their way to avoid fat in their diets, which is healthy—to a point. Yes, too much fat, especially saturated fat, can increase your risk of heart disease, cancer, and obesity. But too little isn't good, either. In fact, your body needs some fat from your diet. After all, dietary fat performs a variety of crucial functions in the body—from making hormones and supplying energy to aiding digestion and promoting the absorption of the fat-soluble vitamins, A, D, E, and K. Plus, fats make eating more pleasurable by adding flavor and texture to foods.

The truth is, the type of fat you consume is as important—if not more so—than the total amount, according to the latest research. The "good" fats include monounsaturated fats, found in olive or canola oils, which reduce artery-clogging LDL cholesterol without affecting HDL (the "good") cholesterol, thereby decreasing your risk of heart disease. Polyunsaturated fats (in seafood and corn oil) also appear to decrease heart disease risk, but some research suggests that the type found in many vegetable oils can increase breast cancer risk. By far the worst fats are the saturated variety (in meats and dairy foods), followed by transunsaturated fats (also called trans-fatty acids), which are found in margarine and baked goods; both of these increase the risk of heart disease.

Most health associations now recommend that you restrict your fat intake to less than 30 percent of your total calories. More specifically, less than 10 percent of the day's calories should come from saturated fat, less than 10 percent from polyunsaturated fats, and up to 15 percent of total calories can be derived from monounsaturated fats. Tracking the fat in your diet has become much easier now that packaged foods bear labels that contain specific nutritional information, including the total and saturated fat content. If you get in the habit of reading labels and checking a fat-gram chart for commonly eaten foods, it's much easier to stick with a healthy eating plan. In fact, people who regularly read nutrition labels eat less fat—approximately 6 percent less, to be exact—than people who don't look at them, according to a study of nearly 1,500 people by researchers at the Fred Hutchinson Cancer Research Center in Seattle.

Water Works

It's not a nutrient, and it doesn't have any calories, but water *is* essential for good health and nutrition. For starters, it's the most plentiful substance in your body, making up 50 to 70 percent of your weight. Not only does simple H_2O carry waste products out of your body, but it aids digestion, regulates body temperature, and lubricates your joints. Drinking adequate amounts of water can also reduce the risks of kidney stones and urinary-tract cancer, according to research. And it can take the edge off your appetite. In fact, many people mistake thirst for hunger and end up eating when what their bodies really want is fluids.

The truth is, many women don't drink nearly as much water as they should. Indeed, many are walking around in a state of mild dehydration. How much is enough? Depending on your level of activity and where you live, your body needs at least six cups of water per day. To make water more palatable, you could add lemon, lime, or orange wedges or make a pitcher of noncaffeine herbal tea. A hidden advantage: If you start getting in the habit of drinking water throughout the day, you'll begin to recognize true hunger when it strikes.

The ABCs of Exercise

Trying to lose weight without exercising is like trying to walk on one leg. Hopping on one foot (or eating less food) could get you to your chosen destination but it's more difficult. You'll get to your goal much more comfortably if you use two legs in concert—in the form of diet and exercise. In fact, in a 1996 study at Baylor College of Medicine in Houston, overweight men and women were divided into three groups. The first group tried to lose weight by following a low-calorie eating plan designed to produce a weight loss of two pounds per week; the second group by exercising five times per week; and the third by combining dietary changes with exercise. After a year, those who followed the diet-only protocol lost twice as much weight as those who simply exercised; those who did both, however, lost the most weight—an average of nearly 20 pounds. Now here's the real surprise: During the second year, the dieting group regained all of the weight they'd lost *plus* an average of two more pounds, whereas those in the exercise-only group and the combination group maintained more of their losses. So exercise appears to make a big difference in sustaining weight loss.

Besides the weight-loss advantage, exercise confers all sorts of health benefits—from lowering your risks of heart disease, cancer, and osteoporosis to boosting your immune system, energy, and state of mind. Exercising regularly will also help you build and maintain muscle mass, which is important for weight control because the more muscle you have, the more efficient your metabolism will be.

What does it really mean to be "fit" these days? The latest definition of physical fitness encompasses three principles—aerobic fitness, strength, and flexibility—each of which requires different forms of exercise. But all three work together to make it easier and more comfortable for you to move through daily activities.

Aerobic exercise, often called cardiovascular conditioning, refers to any sustained activity that uses large muscle groups and is intense enough to challenge—and, hence, condition—your heart and lungs: As you jog, swim, bicycle, or dance over a period of time, your heart starts pumping harder in order to deliver blood and oxygen throughout your body, burning greater

Healthy Eating Habits for Wherever You Dine

If you're trying to lose weight, you may need to shed your old ways of eating and develop some new ones. Here are guidelines that will help you eat healthfully anywhere:

Dining Out

- **Plan ahead.** Before you get to the restaurant, think about what type of item you might order. Also, try not to arrive at the restaurant famished; otherwise, you'll be likely to overeat.

- **Assert yourself.** Don't be shy about asking how dishes are prepared—or about requesting that a dish be prepared without added fat. Surveys have found that the vast majority of restaurants will alter their preparation methods if a customer requests it.

- **Make smart selections.** Whenever possible, order leaner cuts of meat, such as round steak, filet mignon, or center-cut pork or lamb chops. Remove the skin from poultry before eating.

- **Ask for sauce on the side.** Requesting sauce or salad dressing on the side can help you conserve calories. This way, you can control how much goes on the food—by dipping your fork in the dressing, then stabbing the lettuce or a morsel of meat, for example.

- **Break the rules.** You don't have to order courses according to how they're offered. Consider ordering two appetizers instead of one *and* an entree—or sharing a dessert instead of having your own.

amounts of calories and body fat in the process. As a result, your heart and lungs get a good workout, along with your muscles.

For exercise to be truly aerobic, you'll need to work out in your target heart rate zone—between 60 and 80 percent of your maximum heart rate. To calculate your maximum heart rate, subtract your age from 220 (this number reflects your maximum heart rate in beats per minute); next, multiply the resulting number by .60 to figure out the lower limit of your target zone and

EATING AT HOME

• **Drink up.** Have a glass of water or seltzer (if you prefer) while you're cooking dinner or before your meal to take the edge off your appetite. If you drink another glass with your meal, the liquid will help fill you up, making you less likely to overeat.

• **Avoid unnecessary nibbling.** It's a hazard both while you're cooking and cleaning up. Chew gum or suck on a strong mint if you can't resist the urge to nosh while handling food. Similarly, ask a family member or friend to help with the cleanup; this will help you resist the temptation to pick at the leftovers.

• **Eat slowly.** Take time to savor the taste and texture of the food as you chew it. Otherwise, if you eat too quickly, you'll end up eating more because you'll be shortchanging yourself of the sensory experience.

• **Pay attention to what you're eating.** Don't watch TV or do anything else while you're eating. Focus your attention, as best you can, on the food you're putting in your mouth—and enjoy it.

• **Indulge your sweet tooth—in moderation.** Don't deprive yourself of what you crave; instead, treat yourself to a small amount of chocolate—a miniature chocolate bar or a cup of hot chocolate, for instance—or have a fruit-based dessert to top off the meal.

multiply your maximum heart rate by .80 to gauge the upper limit. This range is the intensity bracket within which you should be exercising. Before doing any aerobic exercise, always warm up for 5 to 10 minutes by walking or biking at a gentle pace, then stretching; this will reduce your risk of injury.

Strength training, often referred to as resistance training, does basically what it sounds like: builds muscle strength and mass. You can obtain resistance by moving against gravity if you do sit-ups or push-ups; you can also get resistance from lifting free weights, using machines such as Nautilus, or performing exercises with rubber tubing or Dyna bands. Whatever method you choose, you should use enough resistance so that your muscles feel fatigued after working out; if you feel pain in your muscles, that's a sign that you've overdone it.

If the thought has crossed your mind, don't worry that your muscles will get too bulky if you start strength training. Most women simply do not have the hormones to build such bulging muscles. Women can, however, increase muscle mass, which can, in turn, cause your body to burn calories at a faster rate all the time. That's because each pound of muscle naturally burns 35 to 50 calories a day when you're not exercising; by contrast, a pound of body fat burns only 2 calories a day when you're resting. In fact, building and maintaining muscle mass is one of the best ways to keep your weight stable as you get older, especially since muscle mass declines with age. Strength training can also help prevent bone loss, improve your posture, prevent back problems, and make it easier for you to perform everyday activities more comfortably; recent research also suggests that it may relieve depression. There's no question that it can create more well-defined muscles and give you a more toned appearance.

Flexibility, by contrast, won't trim your waistline or help your metabolism become more efficient. And that may be one of the reasons why it's so often neglected. But it is important. Why? Because developing and maintaining flexibility—whether it's through stretching, yoga, t'ai chi, or other techniques—will help you move through everyday activities and exercise more comfortably, decreasing your chances of injury in the process. It can also help improve your posture. These benefits become especially important as you get older because muscle fibers and tendons naturally shorten with the passing years. As a result, you're likely to lose some of the range of motion you used to have, and you'll become more susceptible to injuries. When you do stretch, be sure to do it to the point where you feel mild tension in your muscles (then hold it for 30 seconds). Don't push a stretch to the point of pain, and never bounce—these strategies can result in injury.

The Exercise Prescription

If you want to get fit and lose weight, you should be exercising in your target zone—at 60 to 80 percent of your maximum heart rate. While it is possible to lose weight by exercising at a lower intensity, you'll have to work out longer (which may be problematic, since many women have a hard time fitting in even short workouts) and you won't reap the maximum fitness benefits from exercise.

How often should you exercise? That, too, depends on your goals. For good health, the U.S. Surgeon General recommends accumulating at least 30 minutes of physical activity on most days of the week. It doesn't have to be vigorous activity, nor does it have to be continuous. Research has found that doing aerobic exercise for three 10-minute stretches offers almost the same health benefits as one 30-minute session. If you want to reap substantial health benefits from exercise, however, many experts recommend that you expend at least 1,000 calories per week in physical activity. You could reach this 1,000-calorie mark by jogging (at the pace of a 9-minute mile) for 30 minutes three days per week or by playing tennis for 45 minutes three times per week (if you weigh 150 pounds).

If you want to lose weight, on the other hand, here's the bottom line: You need to expend more energy through exercise and everyday activities than you take in from food. What this means is you'll need to burn off 3,500 calories more than you consume from food to lose one pound. To make losing weight easier, many experts recommend exercising five times a week—for at least 30 minutes (the longer, the better when it comes to battling the bulge). As a rule, you'll be able to perform weight-bearing activities that involve big muscle groups—walking, biking, and swimming, for example—for longer periods of time, which will help you burn more calories.

Don't be alarmed if the number on the scale doesn't drop immediately. Use your clothes to gauge progress. Chances are, once-snug clothes will start to fit more comfortably within a short period of time. And then you'll know your weight is headed in the right direction.

The Keys to Winning at Weight Loss

In the largest study, so far, of people who have been successful at losing weight and maintaining the loss, researchers from the University of Pittsburgh School of Medicine and the University of Colorado Health Sciences Center have unearthed strategies that work for real people (as opposed to subjects in a study). More than 2,000 women and men have participated in the project, called the National Weight Control Registry, and to qualify for membership, the participants needed to have lost and kept off at least 30 pounds for more than a year. On average, they have maintained their weight loss for more than five years. Approximately 55 percent of participants lost weight with professional assistance or through a formal program such as Weight Watchers, while 45 percent did it on their own.

The vast majority of these dieters had tried to lose weight before but hadn't been successful. What made their last attempt

How to Go for the (Calorie) Burn

The following chart will give you an idea of how many calories you can expect to burn while doing various activities for 30 or 45 minutes. The numbers apply to someone who weighs 150 pounds; if you weigh more, you'll probably burn more calories, and if you weigh less, you'll burn slightly fewer calories in the same time period.

ACTIVITY	30 MINUTES	45 MINUTES
Aerobic dance	276	414
Bicycling	206	308
Cross-country skiing	282	423
Dancing socially	105	158
Gardening	189	284
Golf (if you carry your clubs)	174	261
Golf (if you use a cart)	80	119
Hiking	168	252
In-Line Skating	222	333
Jogging (10-minute miles)	348	522
Racquetball (competitive)	360	540
Running (8-minute miles)	425	637
Skiing (water and downhill)	213	320
Swimming (crawl, moderate pace)	290	434
T'ai chi	144	216
Tennis	222	333
Walking (briskly)	245	367
Weightlifting	245	367
Yoga	144	216

different? While they used a variety of strategies to slim down, sticking with a low-fat, low-calorie diet and exercising regularly were essential to losing weight and maintaining their loss. In one study, 80 percent of the registry participants met or exceeded the recommendation to get less than 30 percent of the day's calories from fat; 35 percent of the participants derived less than 20 percent of their calories from fat. These successful dieters also restricted their intake of certain types of foods and limited their portion sizes of most foods. And they ate frequently throughout the day—nearly five times per day, including snacks.

What may be most significant is nearly every participant used a combination of dietary changes and exercise to lose weight and maintain the loss. Generally, participants engaged in one or two types of physical activity to slim down. Among women, walking, aerobic dance, and bicycling were the most popular choices. And they began exercising frequently and vigorously— reportedly expending more than 2,500 calories per week through exercise, more than twice the usually recommended exercise goal.

One of the most surprising findings: Many participants report that maintaining the weight loss is easier than losing the pounds. Perhaps that's because the payoffs really kick in during the maintenance phase. More than 85 percent of participants report that their physical health and general quality of life have improved and that they have more energy, physical mobility, and self-confidence as a result of losing weight. And many claim that their relationships with other people have improved as well.

Maintaining their slimmer physiques may be easier to do than obtaining them was, but these people haven't shed the diet and exercise strategies that helped them reach their goals. On the contrary, they continue to adhere to their changed ways. If there's one resounding message from these success stories, it's that maintaining weight loss requires an ongoing effort and commitment. Even now, long past their heavy days, most of the successful dieters continue to count calories and fat grams, which suggests that monitoring their own behavior is one of the keys to their success. Nevertheless, they aren't obsessed about their weight. In other words, they don't step on the scale several times a day: 38 percent weigh themselves once a day, 31 percent check their weight just once a week, and 24 percent weigh themselves less often than that.

Because losing a considerable amount of weight can be a long, challenging process, many weight-loss experts emphasize the importance of setting realistic goals. Rather than aiming for your ideal weight, some weight-loss experts believe it's smarter to strive for a weight that's realistic for you. If you want to lose a substantial amount of weight, for instance, you might start with the goal of losing 10 percent of your current body weight; then, when you reach that goal, try to maintain your new weight for a few months to give your body time to adjust to that weight. (Remember: This weight loss alone will lead to significant health benefits.) Once your body has adjusted to its slimmer status, you can try to tackle shedding more pounds if you want to. In any case, congratulate yourself for what you've already accomplished.

The Bottom Line

No matter what stage of life you're in, or what stressful situations you're facing, certain weight-management strategies can be universally helpful—and that's because they work. Here are ten weight-loss secrets to put into practice whenever you find yourself struggling with the scale:

Secret #1

IF YOU WANT TO LOSE WEIGHT, YOU NEED TO EXPEND MORE CALORIES THROUGH EVERYDAY ACTIVITIES AND EXERCISE THAN YOU CONSUME FROM FOOD AND BEVERAGES.

It's really very simple. And the best way to make sure you achieve the right balance is to keep track of approximately how many calories you consume while also logging how many calories you burn off through exercise and other physical activities (such as gardening).

Secret #2

WHETHER YOU GET THEM FROM CARBOHYDRATES, PROTEINS, OR FATS, ALL CALORIES COUNT.

The truth is, every single calorie that enters your body can affect your weight. It's true that some foods are more calorie dense than others, and this is because ounce for ounce or gram for gram, different types of foods supply your body with different amounts of calories. A gram of protein and a gram of carbohydrates each contains comparable amounts of calories (four, to be exact), whereas a gram of fat has more than twice as many (nine calories). So while it's fine—and healthy—to choose from all three food groups, you'll need to pay attention to how many calories are in a serving of each.

Secret #3

DRINKING ADEQUATE AMOUNTS OF WATER IS IMPORTANT FOR LOSING WEIGHT.

Not only does drinking enough H_2O provide all sorts of health benefits, but it can also take the edge off your appetite. The reality is, some people mistake thirst for hunger and end up eating when their bodies really crave fluids. Getting in the habit of drinking at least six cups of water during the day can help you begin to distinguish real hunger from thirst—or simply the desire to put something in your mouth.

Secret #4

EATING REGULARLY—INCLUDING BREAKFAST AND SNACKS—KEEPS YOUR ENERGY HIGH AND HELPS YOU BURN CALORIES MORE EFFICIENTLY.

Many people skip breakfast, in particular, but this is a big mistake. Researchers from the George Washington University School of Medicine in Washington, D.C., have found that people who eat a substantial breakfast, as well as lunch and dinner, burn five percent more calories per day than those who forgo the morning meal.

Secret #5

LOSING WEIGHT WITHOUT EXERCISING WILL HAMPER YOUR PROGRESS.

First of all, you won't burn as many calories as quickly if you don't move your body. Second, by exercising, you'll build muscle, which keeps your metabolism revving high all the time. Third, exercising regularly can help you feel better about yourself, which makes trying to lose weight—or avoid emotional overeating—easier.

Secret #6

BUILDING AND MAINTAINING MUSCLE MASS IS IMPORTANT FOR WEIGHT CONTROL BECAUSE THE MORE MUSCLE YOU HAVE, THE MORE CALORIES YOU BURN.

Each pound of muscle burns 35 to 50 calories a day when you're at rest; by contrast, a pound of body fat burns only 2 calories a day when you're resting. Clearly, burning more calories—both while you're exercising and while you aren't—will help you control your weight. In fact, building and maintaining muscle mass, which tends to decline with age, is one of the best ways to keep your weight stable as you get older.

Secret #7

THE KEY TO MAKING EXERCISE A HABIT IS TO DISCOVER ACTIVITIES YOU ENJOY.

Otherwise, exercise will simply feel like one more chore, one you're likely to shirk whenever you can get away with it. This may be one reason why studies have found that half of people who start an exercise program drop out after just three to six months. It's best to try different activities until you find a couple that suit your preferences and your lifestyle. Also, experiment with different approaches—using the buddy system, joining fitness classes, working with a personal trainer—until you discover what keeps you motivated on a continuous basis.

Secret #8

TO LOSE WEIGHT, YOU'LL NEED TO WATCH YOUR PORTION SIZES, AS WELL AS YOUR FAT AND CALORIE INTAKE.

When it comes to claiming control of your weight, one of the biggest challenges may be curbing the size of your portions. And there's no question: Unless you're a nutritionist, it's not easy to gauge what three ounces of lean beef or a cup of pasta looks like on a plate. What does help is to visualize actual servings of common foods as everyday objects. Here are a few examples of what a serving really looks like:

3 ounces of cooked meat = a deck of cards

3 ounces of fish = one-and-a-half cassette tapes

1 cup of pasta = a tennis ball

1 pancake = a compact disc

2 servings of most breads = a videocassette tape

1 cup of fruit or raw veggies = a baseball

1/2 cup of cooked veggies = a clenched fist

1 ounce of cheese = a pair of dice or a 1-inch cube

1 tablespoon of butter or salad dressing = a half dollar or the tip of your thumb

Secret #9

TO STAY AWARE OF YOUR EATING HABITS, KEEP TRACK OF WHAT YOU EAT AND WHEN IN A FOOD DIARY.

This is often referred to as self-monitoring, and it works because it makes you accountable to yourself for your own behavior. In fact, research has found that keeping a food diary not only can help people control their weight during high-risk holidays but can even help them shed unwanted pounds during these challenging times. If you can't manage to track your eating behavior every single day, doing so three-fourths of the time can also help you shed unhealthy eating habits.

Secret #10

SET REALISTIC GOALS FOR YOUR OWN WEIGHT.

Let's face it: Not everyone can be skinny. But every woman can be fit and look her best. So instead of hoping to become model thin or achieve "an ideal weight," it's smarter to strive for a weight that's realistic for you. If you want to lose a substantial amount of weight, start with the goal of losing ten percent of your current body weight; when you reach it, try maintaining your new weight for a few months to give your body time to adjust. Then you can set your sights on additional weight loss if you need to. But keep in mind that losing ten percent of your weight can make a big difference to your health and well-being.

Your Two-Week Jump Start

It's probably no surprise that the foods you eat can largely affect your success at losing or maintaining your weight, should you find yourself in the midst of one of the Weight Stages. If the task of selecting a variety of satisfying and nutritious foods seems particularly daunting during these phases, our two-week menu, designed for a 150-pound woman, will make planning your daily meals effortless. All 14 days adhere to Weight Watchers **1•2•3 Success Plan** (for more information on the complete plan and how to fit it into your lifestyle, call 1-800-651-6000), including at least five fruit and vegetable servings and two milk servings per day. Whether you're up against the challenges of one of the Weight Stages or simply want to enjoy a more healthful way of eating, the following meal plan can help.

Breakfast

Peach-Crunch Parfait (In an 8-ounce glass, layer one container aspartame-sweetened nonfat vanilla yogurt, 1 cubed medium peach, and ¹/₂ cup low-fat granola cereal.) (6)

Coffee or tea (0)

Lunch

Palm Springs Tuna Pocket (Fill a large whole-wheat pita with ¹/₂ cup each bean sprouts and shredded carrots. Stuff with ¹/₂ cup drained water-packed tuna mixed with 2 teaspoons reduced-calorie mayonnaise and 1 teaspoon each diced red onion and finely chopped dill.) (6)

1 cup cubed mango (1)

1 cup fat-free milk (2)

Snack

1 cup sliced cucumber with 2 tablespoons sour cream and onion dip (2)

Dinner

Sesame Noodles and Vegetables (Heat 1 cup cooked linguine, ¹/₂ cup steamed broccoli florets, and ¹/₂ cup each snow peas and thinly sliced red pepper strips in a nonstick pan with 1 teaspoon each margarine and sesame oil. Remove from the heat and sprinkle with 1 teaspoon sesame seeds and a dash of crushed red pepper flakes; toss.) (5)

1 small glass white wine (2)

1 cup watermelon cubes (1)

TOTAL FOR THE DAY: *25 POINTS*

DAY TWO

Breakfast

1 cup bran flakes cereal (1)

1 cup blueberries (1)

½ banana (1)

1 cup fat-free milk (2)

Lunch

Stuffed Sweet Potato (Top a large cooked sweet potato with ⅓ cup nonfat cottage cheese; sprinkle with 7 chopped walnut halves.) (6.5)

1 cup steamed broccoli florets with 1 teaspoon reduced-calorie margarine (0.5)

Iced mint tea (0)

Snack

1 cup aspartame-sweetened nonfat crème caramel yogurt (2)

Dinner

Blue Cheese Burger (Combine 4 ounces lean ground beef and ¾ ounce crumbled blue cheese. Shape into a patty and broil until cooked through, about 10 minutes. Serve on a light hamburger bun with 1 cup tomato slices and lettuce leaves.) (9)

1 cup steamed zucchini with 1 teaspoon melted margarine (1)

TOTAL FOR THE DAY: 24 *POINTS*

The Secrets of Staying Slim at Any Stage of Life   **169**

Breakfast

Tomato-Egg Melt (Whisk together 2 egg whites, 1 whole egg, and 3 tablespoons shredded part-skim mozzarella cheese; scramble in 1 teaspoon melted margarine; cook until firm. Layer on ½ large onion bagel, top with 1 cup tomato slices.) (7)

1 cup honeydew melon chunks (1)

Coffee or tea (0)

Lunch

Easy Three-Bean Salad (Toss ⅓ cup each cooked black beans and red kidney beans with 1 cup steamed green beans; drizzle with 1 teaspoon each olive oil and red wine vinegar and a pinch each dried oregano and garlic powder.) (3)

1 large pita, toasted and cut into wedges (2)

¼ cup roasted-garlic-flavor hummus (2)

Snack

Berry Delight (In a blender, combine ½ cup each strawberries and raspberries with 1 cup fat-free milk and 3 ice cubes.) (3)

Dinner

Summer Harvest Risotto (Combine ¼ cup arborio rice and 2 tablespoons chicken broth; stir over medium heat for 15 minutes, adding 2 tablespoons more broth as needed. Add ½ cup each chopped summer squash and scallions, 1 teaspoon minced garlic, and ¼ cup broth. Stir until rice is firm. Stir in 2 tablespoons grated parmesan cheese.) (7)

1 cup baby field greens with 2 tablespoons fat-free Italian dressing (0)

1 cup fat-free milk (2)

TOTAL FOR THE DAY: 27 *POINTS*

Breakfast

Cranberry Spice Muffin (Combine ⅓ cup part-skim ricotta cheese, 1 teaspoon granulated sugar, ⅛ teaspoon vanilla extract, and a pinch cinnamon; spread on both halves of a toasted cranberry English muffin.) (5)

1 cup cubed papaya (1)

1 cup fat-free milk (2)

Coffee or tea (0)

Lunch

Pepper-Jack Quesadilla (Layer 3 tablespoons shredded Monterey Jack cheese and 1 sliced medium roasted red pepper between two 6-inch flour tortillas. Microwave on high between two damp paper towels for 2 minutes.) (6)

Chopped Salad (Combine ½ cup each chopped tomato and cucumber; toss with 2 teaspoons lemon juice and 1 teaspoon olive oil.) (1)

1 cup fat-free milk (2)

Snack

1 Bosc pear (1)

Dinner

Herbed Halibut (Coat 8-ounce halibut fillet with 2 tablespoons fresh lemon juice and 1 teaspoon olive oil. Sprinkle with 1 teaspoon each fresh chopped parsley, oregano, and dill; bake at 350°F until fish flakes with a fork.) (5)

1 cup steamed spinach (0)

½ cup cooked brown rice (2)

Raspberry seltzer (0)

TOTAL FOR THE DAY: 25 *POINTS*

Breakfast

Banana-Maple Toast (Whisk together 1 table-spoon fat-free milk, ¹/₈ teaspoon vanilla extract, and a pinch cinnamon; dip 2 slices whole-wheat bread into mixture. Brown in nonstick pan; top with 1 sliced medium banana and 1 tablespoon maple syrup.) (7)

Coffee or tea (0)

Lunch

Peanut Butter and Honey Sandwich (Between 2 slices reduced-calorie whole-wheat bread, spread 1¹/₂ tablespoons reduced-fat peanut butter and 1 tablespoon honey.) (5)

1 cup celery sticks (0)

1 cup fat-free milk (2)

Snack

Yogurt Freeze (In a blender, combine 1 cup aspartame-sweetened nonfat vanilla yogurt with 1 cup frozen peaches or blueberries; serve imme-diately.) (3)

Dinner

Sesame-Soy Beef with Asparagus (In a sealable plastic bag, combine 1 teaspoon each sesame oil, reduced-sodium soy sauce, and minced garlic with ¹/₂ teaspoon each cornstarch and rice wine. Add 6 ounces thinly sliced flank steak; marinate overnight. Spray nonstick skillet with nonstick cooking spray; add beef, marinade, and 1 cup chopped asparagus. Stir-fry until cooked through, 8 minutes.) (7)

1 cup steamed bok choy (0)

1 scoop mandarin orange sorbet (2)

TOTAL FOR THE DAY: 26 *POINTS*

Breakfast

Cheese Danish (In a small bowl, combine ⅓ cup nonfat ricotta cheese, 1 tablespoon sugar, and ¼ teaspoon each cinnamon and nutmeg. Spread onto 2 slices raisin toast.) (6)

1 sliced Granny Smith apple (1)

Coffee or tea (0)

Lunch

Smoked Salmon Wrap (Combine 4 tablespoons nonfat cream cheese and 1 tablespoon chopped dill; divide between two 6-inch flour tortillas. Layer 1 ounce smoked salmon and 1 tablespoon minced onion onto each; roll and secure with a toothpick.) (6)

1 cup mixed greens with fat-free Italian dressing (0)

1 cup frozen seedless red grapes (1)

Snack

3 cups light microwave popcorn (1)

1 cup fat-free milk (2)

Dinner

Baked Scallops (Combine 1 teaspoon each lemon juice and melted margarine, 1 tablespoon white wine, and a pinch of dried thyme; pour over ½ cup scallops. Marinate 20 minutes; bake at 450°F for 5 minutes.) (2)

1 steamed artichoke (0)

Lemonberry Shake (In a blender, combine 1 cup aspartame-sweetened nonfat lemon yogurt with ⅓ cup fat-free milk, 1 cup blueberries, and 3 ice cubes.) (3)

TOTAL FOR THE DAY: *22 POINTS*

Breakfast

Strawberries and Cream Bagel (Top ¹/₂ whole-wheat bagel with 1 tablespoon whipped cream cheese and 1¹/₂ tablespoons strawberry spreadable fruit.) (5)

1 cup aspartame-sweetened nonfat strawberry yogurt (2)

Coffee or tea (0)

Lunch

Make-Your-Own Veggie Burger:

Vegetarian burger (2)

1 light hamburger roll (2)

1 slice low-fat American cheese (2)

Extras: Shredded lettuce, tomato, pickles, onion, mustard, and ketchup (0)

1 cup carrots and celery sticks (0)

1 cup fat-free milk (2)

Snack

1 cup frozen seedless red grapes (1)

Dinner

Salmon BBQ (Combine 1 teaspoon each soy sauce, honey, lemon juice, olive oil, and chopped garlic. Brush on 8-ounce salmon steak; grill 4 inches from heat until cooked through, 5 minutes on each side.) (8)

1 ear of corn (1)

1 cup steamed spinach (0)

1 cup watermelon chunks (1)

TOTAL FOR THE DAY: 26 *POINTS*

DAY EIGHT

Breakfast

1 large fat-free raisin bran muffin with 1 ½ table-
1 ½ tablespoons blackberry spreadable fruit (5)

1 cup mixed fruit (1)

1 cup fat-free milk (2)

Lunch

Honey-Dijon Chicken Sandwich (Combine
1 teaspoon each honey and Dijon mustard;
spread onto 2 slices reduced-calorie whole-
wheat bread and top with 2 teaspoon reduced-
calorie mayonnaise. Top with 3-ounce cooked
skinless boneless chicken breast, 2 slices each red
onion and tomato, and ¼ cup alfalfa sprouts.) (5)

1 cup steamed baby carrots and peas with 1 teaspoon melted butter (1)

Snack

Creamy Cappuccino Freeze (In a blender, combine 1 container aspartame-sweetened nonfat
vanilla yogurt, ½ cup fat-free milk, ¼ cup brewed
espresso, 3 ice cubes, ½ teaspoon superfine sugar,
and ¼ teaspoon cinnamon.) (3)

Dinner

Baked Ziti (Combine 1 cup each cooked ziti
pasta and tomato sauce, ½ cup sliced summer
squash, and 1 teaspoon olive oil. Spread in nonstick baking pan; top with ⅓ cup nonfat ricotta
cheese and 3 tablespoons shredded part-skim
mozzarella cheese. Bake at 350°F until bubbly,
about 15 minutes.) (7)

1 slice Italian bread (2)

1 cup romaine lettuce leaves with 2 tablespoons
fat-free Italian dressing (0)

TOTAL FOR THE DAY: 26 *POINTS*

Breakfast

1 hard-boiled egg with salt and pepper, to taste (2)

1 cup chopped tomato (0)

2 slices whole-wheat toast with 1 teaspoon reduced-calorie margarine (4.5)

Coffee or tea (0)

Lunch

Turkey Club (Toast 3 slices reduced-calorie whole-wheat bread. Layer 1 slice with 2 slices cooked skinless turkey breast, lettuce leaves, tomato slices, and 1 teaspoon mayonnaise. Top with another bread slice; layer with 1/4 cup shredded carrot, 4 cucumber slices, and 1 teaspoon Dijon-style mustard. Top with remaining bread slice.) (6.5)

1 cup fat-free milk (2)

1 cup cantaloupe chunks (1)

Snack

1 container aspartame-sweetened nonfat apple pie yogurt (2)

Dinner

Tofu-Veggie Stir-Fry (Stir-fry 1/3 cup cubed firm tofu and 1/2 cup each chopped mushrooms, bell peppers, broccoli, and carrots in 2 teaspoons vegetable oil until vegetables are tender, about 6 minutes. Stir in 2 teaspoons soy sauce.) (4)

1/2 cup cooked brown rice (2)

1 cup Bing cherries (1)

TOTAL FOR THE DAY: 25 *POINTS*

Breakfast

Sweet Berry Cereal (Top 1 cup cooked cream of wheat cereal with 1 teaspoon each margarine and firmly packed dark brown sugar; sprinkle with 2 tablespoons dried cranberries.) (4)

1 McIntosh apple (1)

Coffee or tea (0)

Lunch

Cheese Nachos (Cut three 4-inch corn tortillas into wedges; toast 5 minutes. Layer with 3 table-spoons shredded nonfat cheddar cheese, ½ cup each shredded lettuce and diced tomatoes, and ¼ cup salsa. Toast until bubbly; top with ¼ cup prepared guacamole.) (7)

1 cup steamed baby corn kernels (1)

Mellow Margarita (In a blender, combine ½ cup Margarita-flavored sorbet and ¼ cup lemon-lime seltzer.) (2)

Snack

1 container aspartame-sweetened nonfat chocolate yogurt with 1 cup fresh strawberries (3)

Dinner

Curried Beef Kabobs (Combine 4 ounces cubed lean beef, 1 quartered small onion, 1 teaspoon vegetable oil, and ½ teaspoon curry powder. Thread beef and onions on a 12-inch skewer and grill or broil 12 minutes, turning occasionally.) (5.5)

1 cup steamed sugar snap peas with 1 teaspoon reduced-calorie margarine (0.5)

1 cup fat-free milk (2)

1 cup fresh raspberries (1)

TOTAL FOR THE DAY: 27 *POINTS*

Breakfast

Maui Muffin (In a blender, combine 1 cup fresh pineapple, $^1/_3$ cup low-fat (1%) cottage cheese, and 1 teaspoon lemon juice until smooth. Spread on an English muffin.) (5)

1 cup aspartame-sweetened nonfat coconut cream pie yogurt (2)

Coffee or tea (0)

Lunch

Mozzarella-Tomato Melt (Layer 3 tablespoons shredded part-skim mozzarella cheese and $^1/_2$ sliced medium tomato between 2 slices pumpernickel bread spread with 2 teaspoons reduced-calorie mayonnaise mixed with $^1/_2$ teaspoon chopped basil; broil until bubbly.) (7)

1 cup baby field greens with 2 tablespoons fat-free Italian dressing (0)

Lemon-lime seltzer (0)

Snack

1 cup fat-free milk (2)

Dinner

Sloppy Joe (In a skillet, cook 4 ounces lean ground turkey, $^1/_4$ cup each chopped onion and red bell pepper, and 1 teaspoon olive oil until turkey is browned. Stir in $^1/_2$ cup tomato sauce, $^1/_2$ minced garlic clove, $^1/_4$ teaspoon chili powder, and dash salt; heat through and serve on a light hamburger roll.) (7)

1 cup steamed green beans (0)

$^1/_2$ cup chocolate sorbet with 1 cup mandarin orange slices (4)

TOTAL FOR THE DAY: 27 *POINTS*

Breakfast

Blueberry Belgian Waffle (Top 1 toasted frozen Belgian waffle with 1 cup blueberries, ¼ cup nondairy whipped topping, and 1 tablespoon maple syrup.) (5)

Coffee or tea (0)

Lunch

Seafood Salad (Halve 1 tomato lengthwise; squeeze out seeds and drain on paper towels for 10 minutes. Combine ½ cup drained cooked orzo pasta, ½ cup imitation crabmeat, ¾ ounce crumbled feta cheese, 10 chopped oil-cured small olives, and 1 teaspoon balsamic vinegar. Stuff into tomato halves.) (7)

½ large pita, toasted (1)

Lemon-lime seltzer (0)

Snack

1 cup fat-free milk (2)

1 banana (2)

Dinner

Vegetable Burrito (Sauté ⅓ cup cooked black beans and ½ cup each chopped tomato, spinach, corn kernels, and chopped mushrooms with 1 teaspoon chopped cilantro and dash each salt and dried onion flakes in 1 teaspoon olive oil. Remove from heat and combine with ½ cup steamed brown rice. Roll mixture in one 6-inch flour tortilla and top with ½ cup each shredded lettuce and salsa.) (6)

Raspberries and Cream Shake (In a blender, combine 1 container aspartame-sweetened non-fat vanilla yogurt, 1 cup raspberries, ¼ cup fat-free milk, and 3 ice cubes.) (3)

TOTAL FOR THE DAY: 26 *POINTS*

Breakfast

1½ cups puffed rice cereal with 1 cup sliced peaches (2)

1 cup fat-free milk (2)

½ cup orange juice (1)

Coffee or tea (0)

Lunch

Shrimp Salad (Combine 1 cup chopped cooked shrimp, ½ cup chopped celery, 2 teaspoons reduced-calorie mayonnaise, 1 teaspoon chopped dill, and 1 teaspoon lemon juice. Serve over 1 cup mixed greens.) (5)

1 slice French bread (2)

½ cup carrot juice (0)

Snack

1 fat-free apple-cinnamon cereal bar (2)

1 cup fat-free milk (2)

Dinner

Sushi Bar Dinner:

1 cup miso soup (2)

1 cup mixed greens with 1 tablespoon ginger-carrot dressing (2)

8 pieces maki sushi (2)

½ cup green tea ice cream (4)

TOTAL FOR THE DAY: 26 *POINTS*

DAY FOURTEEN

Breakfast

Fruit and Cream Cereal (Stir 1½ tablespoons strawberry spreadable fruit into 1 cup prepared cream of wheat; top with 2 tablespoons heavy cream.) (6)

1 cup fruit salad (2)

Coffee or tea (0)

Lunch

Grilled Cheese and Tomato (Layer 2 slices American cheese and 1 slice tomato between 2 slices reduced-calorie whole-wheat bread; broil in toaster oven until bubbly.) (5)

1 cup steamed broccoli (0)

1 can diet cola (0)

Snack

1 cup fat-free milk (2)

2 graham crackers (1)

1 cup grapes (1)

Dinner

Barbecued Chicken (Whisk together 2 teaspoons ketchup, 1 teaspoon each hoisin sauce and cider vinegar, ½ teaspoon molasses, and a dash soy sauce; brush onto a 3-ounce poached chicken breast. Broil 5 minutes on each side.) (3)

Dilled Potato Salad (Toss together 1 cup chopped cooked new potatoes, ½ cup each shredded carrot and chopped scallions, ¼ cup nonfat plain yogurt, 1 teaspoon mayonnaise, and 1 teaspoon chopped dill.) (4)

Diet iced tea (0)

1 cup aspartame-sweetened nonfat black cherry yogurt (2)

TOTAL FOR THE DAY: 26 *POINTS*